Luxembourg Gardens

JOURNEYS OF LIGHT

Chasing the Horizon

Our Adventures Through the British Isles and France

PATRICK & THOMAS KINKADE

HARVEST HOUSE PUBLISHERS
EUGENE, OREGON 97402

Chasing the Horizon

Library of Congress Cataloging-in-Publication Data

Kinkade, Thomas, 1958–
    Chasing the horizon / Thomas and Patrick Kinkade.
        p.   cm.   —(Journeys of light)
    ISBN 1–56507–658–3 (alk. paper)
    1. Europe—Description and travel. 2. Kinkade, Thomas, 1958–
—Journeys—Europe. 3. Kinkade, Patrick, 1959– —Journeys—Europe.
I. Kinkade, Patrick, 1959– . II. Title. III. Series.
D923.K573   1997   97–2662
914.04'55—DC21   CIP
                                                      Rev.

Printed in the United States of America.

Design and production by:
Koechel Peterson & Associates
Minneapolis, Minnesota

97 98 99 00 01 02 03 04 05 06 / DC / 10 9 8 7 6 5 4 3 2 1

To our wives, Laura and Nanette,
whose patience and love give us the strength
to chase all of our horizons.

*(As a tribute to his wife, Thomas Kinkade
has included her initial, N, hidden in
every pencil sketch in the book.)*

Contents

prologue

LIKE MOST JOURNEYS IN LIFE, this one began long before we actually departed.

In truth, it started years ago, and it came about largely because of who my father is and what he instilled in my brother and me.

Dad, you see, is a traveler. If I believed in reincarnation, I'd be convinced he was a gypsy in a previous life. In all my earliest memories he was either traveling or planning to travel or just coming back from traveling. And I say "traveling" as opposed to "being on a trip" because the latter would imply that he had a destination in mind. Dad rarely had one. Whereas someone else might decide to "go to Vancouver," Dad might get an idea to "head north"—wherever the road might take him. Trips were discussed not in terms of sights seen and experiences enjoyed, but as raw accumulation of miles.

"How was your trip, Dad?" I would ask.

"Good, son. I covered seventy-three hundred miles while I was gone."

Dad told me when he retired, "I'm going to follow the sun, son." At the time, I took this to mean he would settle in a warm climate. Now I realize he was announcing his intention to keep on chasing the horizon for as long as he lives. He doesn't just want to lead life; he wants life to lead, and he is always ready to follow. To be confined by itineraries, schedules, and destinations is to miss the true opportunities of the open road and the seduction of what may lie ahead.

Traveling without true destination, of course, has its costs. A traveler may at times be cold, lost, alone, or all three—all mere inconveniences to my father. For him, such discomforts don't even begin to dim the pleasure of following a new interest nor the exquisite lament of leaving pleasant but familiar sights for new ones up ahead.

And so my father travels. He travels passionately. And this wanderlust has been his legacy to my brother and to me.

Admittedly, Dad's wanderings have had a down side for his sons over the years. Dad was not always around when Thom and I were growing up. He and mom parted ways when we were fairly young, and Dad's travels often took him out of our lives for weeks at a time. When we were growing up, our relationship with our father was at best irregular. Dad was no Ward Cleaver, even though my brother and I did bear a striking resemblance to Wally and "the Beav."

And yet . . . there were those times Dad would take us with him on his footloose adventures. And what unforgettable times those were!

In the summer of 1966, I was seven years old, and Thom was eight. And my father, aged forty-eight, was getting ready to hit the road again. It had already become a yearly tradition for Thom and me to join Dad for an adventure on the road, but so far we had only managed to get as far as Disneyland. My brother and I, in fact, often wore our extensive experience with the Magic Kingdom as a badge of honor among our peers. This summer, however, we would be leaving Disneyland far behind. This year we were going to Mexico.

To my father at this time in his life, Mexico was a kind of Shangri-la, a mystical, enchanted place where he was convinced he would find complete contentment. He described it to us as a land of friendly people, good food, and an easy pace. He also mentioned ocean swimming, inexpensive toys, and legal firecrackers. We couldn't wait to go.

We ended up at a small village not far from the Mexican border called Rosarito. I don't know why my father choose this particular place to stop. It could have been the fried lobster dinners for which the town was famous. Or it could have been the beach resort that boasted an evening floor show with a "human sacrifice." Or it could have been some reason all his own. He just stopped, and so did we.

Over the next several days, my brother and I ate roasted pork sandwiches with avocado, won a dance competition at the "Fiesta Mexicana" at a local hotel, and used our arsenal of firecrackers to dynamite every conceivable objet d'art the street venders had to offer. My father did everything and anything he wanted and nothing in particular, content to experience each day as it unfolded. He returned us to our mother sun-browned, the best of friends, and hopelessly addicted to the joy of travel.

More than twenty-five years have passed since the Rosarito trip, and many things have changed. My brother and I have both grown to adulthood and have families of our own.

I am now a university professor, living the relatively genteel life that an academic institution can offer to those who have the calling. My brother, a painter since childhood, has followed his artistic vision to national prominence and critical respect. And my father, now retired, spends most of his time nurturing his beloved Chihuahuas. But many things remain the same—including the wayfarer's itch we all share.

My father has circled America at least five times, traveling almost innumerable miles to tiny, out-of-the-way places to recapture and understand our family history. My brother has hoboed across America on trains and traveled extensively in Europe to develop his signature type of artistic expression. And I have wandered throughout south and central America, the Caribbean, and Europe gathering eccentric experience for its own sake while both worrying and amusing an exceptionally understanding wife.

We have all stayed in five-star hotels and slept in bus stations. We have eaten dishes prepared by world-renowned chefs and have taken our meals from vending machines or soup kitchens. We have experienced the sublime and silly, the majestic and mundane. We have survived physical dangers and exhaustion and have grown from the experiences. Through it all, we have been spiritually touched by the beauty of much of the world and have been rewarded by many unforeseen and unexpected kindnesses. Indeed, all three of us have returned from our journeys already thirsty to go again.

And so, in 1995, we gave in once more to the call of the road. It had long been a dream of Dad's to revisit some of the places where he had been stationed during World War II. Both my brother and I were eager to spend time with our dad and perhaps recapture some of that camaraderie we enjoyed on that long–ago trip to Mexico. I also wanted to explore some of the same country I enjoyed on my honeymoon, while Thom desired to engage in his favorite practice of plein–air painting—creating impressionistic works in oil completely on site and in a flurry of artistic inspiration.

We were gone from our families and our lives for almost two weeks, and apart from an appointment in Ireland we had relatively little idea where we would be going or staying.

And, yes, there were times when we were lost, cold, and alone. We would have had it no other way. As risking allows one to win, so traveling allows one to experience.

My father taught that to Thom and me. And we have grown to believe him.

For my part,
I travel not to go anywhere,
but to go. I travel for travel's sake.
The great affair is to move.

ROBERT LOUIS STEVENSON
Travels with a Donkey

I

Reunion at IvyGate

I ARRIVED IN NORTHERN CALIFORNIA on a cool and clear evening after a relatively short flight from my home in Fort Worth. Thom had planned to pick me up at the airport, but he became tied up with a print signing that had to be completed before we left for Europe. In his stead, he sent his regular driver and a stretch limousine.

A stretch limousine. This may have been business as usual for a man in the public eye such as my brother, but not for me. In fact, at this point of my life, I had been in a limousine exactly twice.

The first time involved a friend's bachelor party. A group of us had arranged for this transport to avoid any legal transgressions that might result from over-exuberant male bonding. The second occasion was the trip between the church where I was married and the reception hall where my wedding party would be held. This time the intention was to avoid any possible legal transgression resulting from over-exuberant husband-and-wife bonding.

In both cases, that limo represented simple, if spacious transportation. Now, however, I was alone in the back of a car that might have been designed to haul the offensive line of a professional football team. And this vehicle, unlike those earlier ones, was fully equipped. I had at my disposal comforts that are rarely available in homes, let alone automobiles: a remote control television with satellite uplink, a video player complete with video library, a cordless phone, and an electric powered revolving pantry with hot and cold running snacks.

I am not suggesting that the experience was unpleasant, but it was bit overwhelming, a bit surreal. I *firmly* believe it should be peculiar to anybody's mindset that luxury hotel rooms can travel down a freeway at sixty-five miles an hour.

The driver on this particular trip was a Filipino gentlemen in a dark suit and sunglasses nicknamed Cookie. By his own account he had been driving as a chauffeur for several years. Given his occupation and what appeared to be a natural talkativeness, I decided to exploit him for insight into what must assuredly be the flamboyant lifestyle of those who use his service.

"So, anything really wild ever happen while you were driving?" I asked. For intimacy's sake I opened the "talk-through window" and declined to use the intercom.

"Oh, no, sir. We've never had any trouble," Cookie responded.

Undaunted and unbelieving, I pursued the topic. "Have you ever had a celebrity in your car?"

Without hesitation he answered, "Just your brother, sir. Everybody around here knows him."

It is an unsettling experience to realize that a sibling has reached celebrity status within his field. To be sure, there is a sense of pride, but there is also that sense of strangeness.

Imagine waking one morning and walking to the mirror. You splash water on your face to wash away the sleep. You look up, expecting your own reflection, and you find Billy Carter looking back at you. Or Roger Clinton.

No, I am not the brother of a president, but discovering myself to be the brother of "Thomas Kinkade, Painter of Light" is still a revelation. I smile when I think of my own recognition of this fact. A friend of mine once suggested that I trademark a title for myself.

Yes, that's me: "Patrick Kinkade, Brother of Light."

When I arrived at IvyGate, my brother's studio, Thom was just finishing up his signing. For those who have not known Thom since childhood, the scene may have held some incongruities.

My brother the artist, you see, was signing prints in a well-worn, brown leather motorcycle jacket—bought in homage to the oversized vintage "hog" he keeps in his garage and on which he roars up and down the coast of California. In the corner of the room a video was playing—a collection of spills and thrills taken from raceways around the country. While tires screamed and gas tanks exploded across the room, my brother was meticulously signing and noting the last fifty prints of a canvas depicting a lovely rustic cottage with warmly glowing windows.

But there was no inconsistency to that scene in the studio. It was simply Thom pursuing an interest, fulfilling an obligation, sincerely enjoying himself, and, as is typical, doing it all at once. Besides, a fascination with racecar wrecks has long been a Kinkade family tradition.

My father was also sitting in the room talking with one of my brother's assistants. As Dad had been prone to do since my brother first suggested this adventure, he was reminiscing about "the war." As Thom was prone to do, he was giving my father raised eyebrow looks.

To Dad, conversation seems to be merely a flow of non sequiturs—an outpouring of unrelated bits of information spewing out of him like a volcano pouring out fine ash. Thom told me later that Dad's contributions up to this point had included observations about a WWII aircraft called the "Mosquito Bomber," the medical system, his recent operation, and the size of an Indian hogan a friend built in the desert. On the last topic Dad was especially lucid; the person in question apparently had managed to create with his own hands an adobe shack roughly the size of an eight-wide mobile home, though with the advantage of a central firepit. Dad's overriding comment was his inevitable, "Well, to each his own, son."

My father is every inch his own man. In looking at him, one can easily recognize the years and miles he has managed to live through. The character lines on his face are deep with personality, and the arch in his back reflects the toll the passage of time can take.

His ever-present baseball cap hides thinning hair, his belt has been loosened a few notches since he last fit into his army uniform, and he is on his second set of knees, the first ones having worn out from heavy use several years ago. Yet, my father's heart still beats young, and his soul is ageless. I know of no one else who, with even fewer years, would be willing to travel as my brother and I had planned. Dad has aged but he will never become old.

I interrupted the conversation and my brother's work with my usual salutations. Thom glanced up, smiled, and barked our traditional greeting—"All right!" The acknowledgment apparently flawed the signing in some way; he scratched the print and tossed it to the floor on a relatively large pile of rejects. My brother has very high standards for something I personally have never considered establishing a standard for—the presentation of a signature.

My father also smiled and added his greeting. Taking a deep breath, I plunged in. The journey had officially begun.

"How is everyone in Sacramento, Dad?"

/ DAD'S "GIRLS"

"Oh, Boo Boo and Chi Chi are fine." These are my father's Chihuahuas. Knowing that I had probably been referring to our human relations in Sacramento, my brother shook his head and chuckled. Knowing that to distract my dad from stories of his beloved "girls" would be a difficult, if not an impossible task, I sat back for the story.

For better or worse, Dad is Dad.

For better or worse, Thom and I both learned that a long time ago.

———————◇———————

When I awoke the next morning, another limo was waiting to drive us from IvyGate to San Francisco International airport. Thom's wife, Nanette, and his two small daughters, Merritt and Chandler, were also up to see us off. The affectionate farewell was punctuated by some nervousness because Nanette, well into her third pregnancy, had experienced some unusual contractions a couple of days earlier. The doctors had been reassuring, however, and she and Thom had agreed in faith to continue with the travel plans. Fortunately, baby Winsor would delay her arrival until after we returned.

With a final hug, my brother tossed his "rolling studio"—a combination easel and carrying case he had designed himself—into the trunk of the car, and we were on the road by seven-thirty that morning. Our plane was not scheduled to leave until one that afternoon, but we had a couple of important stops to make before we could go to the airport.

Most important, we had to secure a new passport for Thom.

It never ceases to amaze me that a document that comes up for renewal every ten years will inevitably expire the day before it is needed. Moreover, its expiration will not be discovered until just that point in time. This, of course, was the predicament in which my brother found himself. A few calls to the State Department, however, had revealed that San Francisco was one of two cities in California that does have a same-day passport issuance service. Relieved, we simply planned to stop at the passport office on our way to the airport.

We arrived there at nine o'clock, four hours before our departure. Plenty of time, we thought, especially in the early spring, which is off-season for the American traveler. But when we arrived and saw the two-hundred-foot long line in front of the passport window, we began to question our judgment. After a wait of more than an hour, Thom managed to talk to a clerk, who informed us that the earliest the document could be ready was at one-thirty—half an hour after our scheduled departure! While Dad and I retired to a nearby coffee shop to think out some other options, Thom stayed in the office and experienced what he typically refers to as "an everyday miracle."

It is important to know this about my brother. He expects good things to happen, and by God's grace they almost always do.

This time, he happened upon a second clerk who was willing to find a supervisor who in turn was willing to forego protocol and hurry the application through the necessary channels. Once the wheels were turning, Thom went to find Dad and me at our table. A Cheshire Cat grin spread across his face as he shrugged, "They'll have it by eleven-thirty."

That left plenty of time to walk up the street, finish our errands, and get a few necessaries for the trip.

First stop was a stationery store, where my brother stocked up on pens, portable leads, retractable pencils, pencil holders, and the like, so that after our visit his pockets resembled those of a fifties-era engineer.

Next stop was a local pipe and tobacco shop. Since neither my brother, my dad, nor I are smokers, this second stop probably bears some explanation.

When traveling, you see, both Thom and I have taken to occasionally adopting an image or persona for the journey.

For example, I once traveled the entire length of the country dressed as the character Hawkeye Pierce from the television show M.A.S.H.—military fatigues, a tee shirt, an open Hawaiian over-shirt, and a cowboy hat—simply to experience onlooker reactions.

More recently, for a trip to San Diego, my brother and I had taken on the personas of two high-rolling businessmen from New

Tintern Abbey

Jersey. At that time, because we felt it fit the image that we were portraying as the "Kinkades from Bensonhurst," we had taken to chomping cigars, tipping big, and carrying on conversations such as:

"Yo, Vin-nie!"

"Ya, Sal!"

"Am I right?"

"Sal, when you're right, you're right!"

Sal (Thom), Vinnie (me), and Dad had stayed at the Hotel del Coronado in San Diego during this particular adventure. The "Hotel del" is a posh beach resort built in the 1930s and used as the backdrop to the film *Some Like It Hot*. In a typical Kinkadian twist of events, Vinnie and Sal stumbled into Tony Curtis in the hotel's lobby. "Hey, Tony, dis is Vinnie," crowed my brother as he introduced me to his new pal Tony. "And this is Dad."

"Hi, ya, D-a-a-d!" Tony Curtis said with a hint of irony to the man, roughly his own age, who stood before him.

My brother was on a roll.

Other images adopted over the years included my brother's corncob pipe-smoking, Depression-era hobo. This character took a cross-country trip with fellow artist James Gurney to collect material for the book *An Artist's Guide to Sketching*. Thom also adopted a rustic burl pipe in honor of Norman Rockwell during a two-week painting excursion to Rockwell's hometown of Arlington, Vermont.

In travel, as in show business, image is everything.

So as we departed for Europe, the quiet whisper of a fine English briarwood pipe could not be denied. A warming draft of fine English shag tobacco on a foggy evening conjured up memories of Sherlock Holmes—even if it would make us cough and wheez.

So passport in hand, unlit pipe in mouth, and images of England dancing through our heads, we flew out of San Francisco right on schedule.

All the world's a stage,
and all the men
and women merely players;
They have their exits and their entrances;
And one man in his time
plays many parts.

WILLIAM SHAKESPEARE
As You Like It

A Few Miles Above Tintern Abbey

A FRIEND AND I ONCE SPENT THE NIGHT in the central train station of Rome. By three o'clock in the morning, what had been a room full of happy vacationers turned into a way station for lost souls. The discomforts of the sleeping arrangements coupled with the undeniable truth that no one sleeps attractively created such a disheveled mass of humanity that the group as a whole became horrific.

Arriving at London's Heathrow Airport approximately twelve hours after we had left San Francisco had much the same effect on myself and my fellow travelers.

International flights are, without a doubt, the closest thing to purgatory that a human being should ever have to experience. The seats were cramped, the air was stuffy, and the feeling one got when attempting to move around can, at best, be described as strangled.

Moreover, when we first boarded the plane, after being forced to check several of our "carry-on bags," we proceeded to fill to overflowing the compartments above our seats. In fact, our allotted overheads were so full that many of our travel essentials spilled over into our seats. The result was that scattered about us on this 747, in addition to the usual magazines and air sickness bags, was a books-on-tape version of *The Sun Also Rises*, jackets, sunglasses, Thom's sketching easel, a bag containing recording equipment, various cameras, and small nylon rucksacks filled with wallets, travelers' checks, papers, passports, and countless other "essential" articles. This mountain of travel material spread around us like flack from a detonated grenade.

So much for traveling light.

When the vacuum seal popped on the airplane door and the passengers began to move onto the walkway, Thom, Dad, and I were more than ready to disembark.

Thom and I got through customs with very little difficulty. A quick answer to the "what are you going to be doing in this country" and "how long are you going to be staying" questions was enough to appease the British customs officers.

My father, on the other hand, has always had the knack of running into trouble with such gatekeepers.

Dad had given all of his luggage to Thom to carry through the airport, and the agents were apparently questioning my father about the incongruity between his lack of luggage and his declared intent to stay in England "a couple of weeks." As in the past, Dad was about to invoke his mystical and to this day unclarified relationship with the Sacramento County Sheriff's Department to intimidate his inquisitioners. And the Customs officers, for their part, seemed ready to do a strip search.

Thankfully, neither side had to pull their ace to resolve the situation. My brother intervened, sparing the British government a confrontation between their military and my dad's sheriff buddies and sparing the rest of us the sight of my father naked.

"Dad," I smiled, "you have to stay out of trouble!"

"Ah, son, I don't know," he reflected—a familiar punctuation mark for many of the experiences we have had while traveling.

On a whim, but at Dad's suggestion, we decided to make Stonehenge the first stop in our travels. Thom had already made arrangements for us to visit in Ireland—one of our few planned stops—with his colleague David Winter, world-famous for his sculpted reproductions of quaint cottages. The monument would serve as a natural way station on this particular leg of our journey.

John Aubrey, who first described Stonehenge in the seventeenth century, gave it great notoriety as a religious monument built by the

Druids, the holy men of the ancient Celtic tribes that once inhabited the region.

These claims, though, have long since been discredited by the discovery that the ruins predate the time of the Celts in England by several hundred years. Yet even now, the concentric rings of monolithic stones continue to inspire bizarre explanations about their origins.

The most fanciful of these—and the one I find most personally appealing—suggests that the stones were transported from Ireland and magically erected as a tribute to Arthur, the once and future king of England, by Merlin the magician. Another theory, which shares approximately the same amount of credibility, would have it that the stones were put in place by space aliens. Still other stories have attributed Stonehenge's origin to a race of giants, to the Atlantians (of Lost Continent fame), and to the lost tribes of Israel.

If the truth be known, however, it is a mistake to think of Stonehenge as a single site and of single creation. It is more likely a series of constructions built over many years. And geologic analysis has shown that the stones were not brought from Ireland or outer space but from Wales.

Our personal experience with Stonehenge began as we were motoring west from London toward Dartmoor. I would assume that anyone driving the road between these two endpoints would share our initial impression, which was, quite frankly, one of disappointment. Because the plains of Salisbury are vast and open and offer unobstructed horizons, you see Stonehenge well before you reach it, and the initial impact is greatly diminished.

The experience of Stonehenge, however, is not as much a matter of view as feeling. To circle the stones on foot with the winds of the flatlands whistling through their intricate pattern is to get a sense of this ageless mystery.

Actually, this was not my first visit to the site. In fact, I would recommend the approach of my earlier visit to gain the optimum feel for Stonehenge.

Several years ago, three friends and I were driving out from
Oxford, and we decided the monument would be worth investigating. As things go with such irregular forms of travel, we arrived
well after dark on a cloudy night. The night's darkness and the overcast weather acted as a blanket to cover the stones until we drew
close on foot. Then we saw Stonehenge as if an artist had unveiled
it: stark and dramatic.

The gates to the footpath circling the site were closed and locked,
so we bribed a guard to let us in. We were alone at the site and able
to leave the marked trail and walk among the pillars. For more than
an hour we sat and talked, picked the small yellow flowers that grow
around the base of the stones, and basked in the history of the location. It was a haunting experience.

This time around, we remained at Stonehenge for the better part
of an hour, while Thom produced a pencil sketch of the monument and
my father argued with a gate guard about re-entry to the site without a ticket. Before Dad's honorary sheriff's badge could be produced,
I disentangled him from his newest adversary and we left the mythic
stone circle behind, heading for the typical park service stucco snack bar.

It occurs to me that no matter where I've traveled in the indus-
trialized West, some park official invariably feels these small buildings offer just the right touch to any historically or spiritually
enlightening location. British rangers were no different. Nonetheless,

Stonehenge

a lunch of chicken and sweet-corn sandwiches and "Stonehenge rings"—heavily chocolated donuts—was obtained, and we were off.

If you're interested in an intimate experience with the stones without the need for a bribe and a midnight drive, I did question an official-looking fellow about the possibility of walking through the monument as opposed to simply around it. He said they do occasionally let down the chains for the general public, most notably during the summer solstice. The practice started as the result of "The Battle of the Beanfield," as he called it. In the late 1980s, a group of modern-day druids converged on Stonehenge intent on occupying it for their "holy day." A confrontation erupted between this group and a police contingent that had been dispatched to protect the monument. The net result of the "battle" was the official recognition of Stonehenge as a place of worship.

The lesson, then, is that if you desire a close look at the stones, you should wrap yourself in gauze, put flowers in your hair, and chant. If what my acquaintance told me is true, chances are you will be let right in.

As we traveled north from Stonehenge across the English countryside, several things become apparent about the British and about Britain.

The first is that the country has a fascination with road crossing signs.

An hour out from Stonehenge, I had counted seven different varieties of signs. These, of course, included the more familiar types such as "Deer Crossing" and "Livestock Crossing," but also moved into the more eccentric—"Duck," "Tank," and—my personal favorite—"Elderly Crossing." One gets the image of free-ranging flocks of senior citizens closing roads with their migratory patterns.

The second insight has to do with the British sense of style. While it is true that tweeds are still at the height of fashion in the

Man With
Muttonchops
ENGLAND

British countryside and that the racing cap is commonly worn, these clothing choices are generally acceptable to the eye of the American onlooker. However, the fact that "mutton chops" whiskers remain in vogue will eventually drive the American sensibility to distraction. Except in Victorian engravings and old film footage of sixties psychedelic bands, I am convinced one will not see an odder collection of facial hair arrangements anywhere on earth.

The final observation has to do with the town pub. My brother jokes that the only two things you are guaranteed to find in any town in the British countryside is a church and pub, and it is a coin toss as to where you are more likely to find the parish clergy.

To be fair, the image and use of the village tavern does not seem to parallel that of the American neighborhood bar. The "pints" that are drawn by the patron of the pub are consumed with more moderation than those that are typically imbibed in American bars, and the atmosphere is more family oriented. Indeed, it is a charming fact of everyday life in these small hamlets that the pub is not only a central meeting place and civic hall for an area's locals but is also the chief source of news and entertainment, replacing the American television.

In the British countryside the art of the conversation is not dead; people talk and tell stories and listen intently while others are enjoying their turn. It is clearly a great loss if the wayward traveler does not take advantage of the friendly discourse that occurs in the country pub. This was not a loss my brother and I wanted to incur on our first day in England.

Devizes was the first town where we decided to stop. This quaint village was particularly appealing because the well-attended pub that we spotted was situated next to a series of thatched-roof cottages, any of which could serve as the perfect subject for one of Thom's on-the-spot oil sketches.

These small dwellings had a magical look to them. If they were not survivors from a different era, they had at least been created to look that way. Although none of them seemed to be anything but a private dwelling, each had a copper nameplate attached to the gated pathway that led up the front door. Thom quickly found a vantage spot to set up his portable studio while Dad and I strolled down the lane, gazing at the warm lights of Jasmine Cottage, Apple Tree Cottage, Stonechat Cottage, Old Well Cottage, and Horsesill Well.

After the painting was completed and my father was soundly napping in the front seat of our car, Thom and I headed into the

George Inn. As we settled into our seats, I conjured up images of C.S. Lewis and J.R.R. Tolkien sharing conversation and a pint at the Eagle and Child tavern in Oxford. Somehow a pint in a pub seems so thoroughly British.

Although Thom and I had clearly drawn the curiosity of the tavern regulars, we for the most part kept the conversation between ourselves. We had been on the run almost since my arrival at IvyGate and had not really had the opportunity to spend any time in private conversation—a rarity in any circumstance given our current life directions. As is typical, the discussion turned quickly to reminiscence.

I am not sure if it is a common feeling or not, but I often miss the people I care about most intensely when they are sitting right in front of me. I think it is because the responsibilities of everyday living can be so distracting that I don't even realize they have been absent from my life for so long. Being back with Thom reminded me of all the warmth my family provided me, the youngest, as I was growing up. I left that pub that day fed by more than just lunch.

It was time to head toward Wales, where we hoped to spend the night—with only one major stop on the way.

———————◇———————

I was sixteen and my brother was seventeen when we first came under the influence of the senior English teacher of El Dorado High School. Thom and I both spent a full year under Gordon Purdy's tutelage, and both of us, during our tenure in senior English, acquired a Purdy-bestowed nickname. Thom, for some reason, became "Hambone," and I, as was typical to much of my educational experience, became "Thom's little brother."

Mr. Purdy had a reputation of being a strict, humorless academician. He taught British literature, it was said, as if it were the thing worth knowing in the universe. He was a genius at challenging his students and infecting them with a deep reverence for the written word. I mention this because Gordon Purdy was partly responsible for the choice of our next stop. My semester project in Mr. Purdy's class involved an in-depth analysis of the poetry and prose of William Wordsworth. In particular I had to comment on one of the poet's most notable pieces of work, a poem entitled "Lines Composed a Few Miles above Tintern Abbey."

If you are traveling in south Wales, irrespective of whether or not you are a survivor of Mr. Purdy's senior English, head toward Tintern and explore the abbey. By chance Thom and I noticed its proximity to our eventual destination, and so off we headed on the trail of one of the great Romantics.

We arrived in Tintern in the late afternoon. The weather was crisp and clear, and the sight of the abbey nestled far below us in the green valley of the Wye River took my breath away. Even at a distance, the ruined buildings loomed far larger than I had imagined, and their majesty was matched by the dramatic sweep of the landscape.

Before we were to explore this area, however, my brother suggested we stop for a "cream tea." I had never heard of such a thing, and when I questioned Thom about it, he would only smile and say, "Nanette and I had several the last time we were in England. Don't worry. You'll like it."

I liked it.

A cream tea is a joy to the palette of anyone who loves good food and, without a doubt, the worst nightmare of any cardiologist. It amounts to a quality tea served piping hot along with crisp, buttery scones and a heavily sugared substance that is somewhere between cake icing and whipped cream. Think of it as a homemade strawberry shortcake without the influence of anything so healthy as fruit. A British tea time will never inspire the same image for me again.

After far too much tea and too many scones, Thom, Dad, and I set about our explorations. My brother was going to set up his easel at a point high above the abbey to capture it in oil in the fading light. My father wanted to explore the ruins and the town of Tintern itself, and I decided to spend some time at the abbey and then hike the hills as Wordsworth had done the century before.

Tintern Abbey was founded in 1131 by an order of Cistercian monks. The ruins that are visible in the valley, however, were built in the thirteenth and fourteenth centuries. The roofs of the buildings were removed as part of Henry VIII's power struggle with the Roman Catholic church in the sixteenth century. Yet the abbey's general structure remains intact—a tribute, perhaps, to the strength of the sacred over the secular, or to the skills of its fourteenth-century builders. The abbey ruins are characterized by immense but empty Gothic windows, stories high in construction, and vast worship spaces through which sunlight beams in luminescent pillars.

Despite the buildings' awesome architecture, however, the "lines" of Wordsworth were not actually inspired by the abbey. It was the natural grandeur of the Wye River valley that moved Wordsworth to write the poem and his ruminations on man's spiritual relation to God's creation that guided its completion. As I set out for my explorations, I began to gain a clearer sense of why this particular spot inspired him so.

On this walk though wooded hills, I skirted cliffs that plunge into the river on one side and enjoyed vistas of rolling green farmland on the other. Wildflowers and wildlife were in abundance. I was moved to watch a pair of swans floating silently down the river, enjoying both their lifelong union and the tranquillity of the day.

I walked on to what the locals call the Devil's Pulpit. This large stone outcropping, shaped roughly like a preacher's pulpit, commands an unsurpassed view of the valley and the abbey ruins. Although the devil is said to have tempted the monks from this stone as they labored in the fields below, I am inclined to doubt the tale. Surely the vista would have left even the Prince of Lies speechless.

This was not the first time I had been involved in a "Wordsworth hunt." While on our honeymoon, my wife, Laura, and I had visited

Dove Cottage in England's lake district, the quaint dwelling where the poet wrote his most important body of work. I even snatched an opportunity, while the tour guide continued into another room, to have my picture taken in the poet's writing chair. Laura still shudders at that minor act of subversion, but I have never regretted it. My impulsiveness was due in part to my desire to capture a sense of Wordsworth's spirituality—the same motivation that drove me on this silent walk high above this beautiful valley.

DEVIL'S PULPIT,
RIVER WYE, AND
TINTERN ABBEY

The poet viewed humans, nature, and the divine as inseparable and in consonance with each other during times of solitary reflection. Wordsworth in the Wye, Ansel Adams in Yosemite, and Henry David Thoreau at Walden Pond all depicted the same soulfelt awareness of the majesty of nature. Because God created the beauty of nature, they believed, so could one touch the Creator's face by allowing a moment for the spirit to appreciate the earth and sky and all that each contain.

I loved that time in the valley, and I enjoy my brother's oil of Tintern Abbey all the more because of it. Like Wordsworth's poem, Thom's canvas mingles natural beauty, human achievement, and spiritual yearning, sifting them through the artist's unique sensibility and fusing them inseparably in the mind of the viewer. Can any artist—painter or poet—aspire for more?

And I have felt
A presence that disturbs me with the joy
Of elevated thoughts; a sense sublime
Of something far more deeply interfused,
Whose dwelling is the light of setting suns,
And the round ocean and the living air,
And the blue sky, and in the mind of man:
A motion and a spirit, that impels
All thinking things, all objects of all thought,
And rolls through all things.

WILLIAM WORDSWORTH
Lines Composed a Few Miles above Tintern Abbey

III

Tripping an Irish Jig

WE HAD STAYED THAT NIGHT in Haverfordwest, the last area of any real population before the port town of Fishguard, the departure point for the ferry to Ireland. Our idea was to enjoy a good night's rest at a decent hotel, then proceed down what seemed an inconsequential last few miles of road to catch the ferry at six the next morning.

I awoke with a start. My room phone was ringing. I glanced at my watch and realized I had not kept it current to all of the time zone changes we had flown or driven through the previous day. My watch told me it was still yesterday. I groaned and reached for the receiver.

"Son, get up. We're late." Somehow I had known Dad would be on the other end of the line.

"Dad, how can we be late? The ferry doesn't leave for another two hours. . . ." My eyes were finally focusing on the clock atop the room television.

"Well, son . . . the hours we gained back by driving west after losing hours flying east were relost by daylight savings' time."

Although I felt "Huh?" was the natural response, I instead mumbled something about being right down and hung up.

Being an experienced traveler, I have an uncommon capacity for showering, shaving, dressing, and packing in a very short period of time. That morning, I was truly amazing. I moved through that hotel room in ways that did not seem humanly possible. Ten minutes after receiving Dad's call, I was downstairs throwing my luggage into the trunk of our car. Thom was waiting behind the wheel, tweed cap upon his head, smile beaming brightly. Dad was snoring loudly in the backseat.

"When did you find out we lost an hour?" I looked over to Thom as I settled into the navigator's position in the front of the car.

"I guess Dad called me right after he finished talking to you." He smiled and added, "What kept you?"

Popping the car into gear, we bolted into the street and the early tracings of the day's dawn. "Huh?" seemed as if it were going to turn into a theme for the day.

The ferry was still at the dock when we roared into the ticketing facility. We had made it with five minutes to spare; Thom would be able to keep his appointment with David Winter.

We drove onto the "SeaLynx," secured the car, walked up to the ship's restaurant, and made ready for the cruise.

A "cruise," however it was not. That word conjures up the image of a leisurely, relaxed sea crossing. The "Lynx" was anything but leisurely. An unholy mix between hydroplane and oil tanker, this high-speed craft is designed to make the three-and-a-half hour trip between Fishguard and the Irish town of Rosslare in an hour and a half. We soon found out that the tradeoff for great speed is an exceedingly rough ride. The SeaLynx travels high in the water and provides its passengers with an exceptionally acute feel for the wave action through which it is passing—and with a sixty-mile-per-hour headwind there was quite a bit of wave action.

Several of our shipmates, in fact, became "unsettled" just a few minutes out from port. Thankfully, we Kinkades are a stout lot, and the sights, sounds, and smells of our less seaworthy fellows did little to distract us from a hearty breakfast of chicken salad sandwiches and egg-and-bacon "baps"—a sort of British Egg McMuffin.

After finishing our meal, we set about exploring our ship. There were the typical "duty free" shops, an onboard pub (surprisingly

Wickworth Cottage

well-attended at 9 A.M.), and even a few slot machines. But the only thing the boat was really designed to provide its passengers was speed, which was provided in abundance. To the delight of my brother and myself, we were allowed to enjoy the effects of its high velocity up close and personal. Indeed, after casually stepping through a yellow bulkhead door with the words *Extreme Danger* painted at its center, Thom, Dad, and I were let out directly onto the open bow of the ship.

Immediately a strong feeling of vertigo struck; we must have been a hundred feet above the water's surface. The boat's bouncing contributed to the sense of personal disequilibrium, and the wind blast was truly frightening. As we walked into the air current, our bodies sloped forward at an unnatural angle and our tearing eyes eventually had to avert. At this point I noticed with some concern that only a slim rail stood between us and the ice-blue waters of the English South Sea.

I found it astounding that my father, who has two artificial knees, was still with Thom and me when we reached the very point of the ship's bow. I was even more astonished that the liability of allowing passengers onto this open section of the boat had not closed down the line years ago.

As the three of us hung onto the rail and enjoyed the gale force air in our faces, we were joined by yet a fourth intrepid soul. He would not come out to the railing, probably for the reasonable fear of being pitched over the side, but he did beckon us back toward him and the relative shelter of the breezeway. My father made his way back to our new acquaintance while Thom and I just hung on. After several minutes of talking, hand gestures, and back-slapping, my father returned to the rail.

"He just wanted to know if we wanted our picture taken," Dad explained, shaking his head, "Another crazy American!"

He was, but the pictures turned out well anyway.

We pulled off the ferry at Rosslare Harbor a short ninety minutes after we had left Wales.

"Where are we heading?" I asked my brother.

"Toward Thomastown in County Kilkenny," he answered with a smile.

"Thomastown?"

"A coincidence, really."

"Fine, but if I see a sign for Nanetteshire, you are going to have some explaining to do." Thom nodded agreement and turned on the main road heading west.

———————◇———————

We were driving on a one-lane road through farming country, rising to hilltops with vast vistas of the green rolling landscape, then dipping into valleys with tall hedgerows dividing the fields. The drive was exhilarating, especially when occasional cars heading the opposite direction would confront us, often with no slowdown, and force us into the bushes.

We made several wrong turns along the way, each of which delighted us as we came upon some new and unexpected view. At one point we passed by a vast stone ruin and were overwhelmed at how it dominated the landscape. On another road we drove through a stone village consisting of a small Catholic church and a pub, around which were gathered several cottages and farmhouses. As we passed, services had just ended and a group of townspeople were filing out of the church and into the pub. The universal reaction of every face as we drove past was one of surprised suspicion—the raising of the eyebrows, the questioning glance. We were clearly outsiders, especially since our car featured English plates.

It was going to be an interesting couple of days.

I had never met David Winter, his manager, John Hines, or any of the Winter clan prior to that day, but they all were the sort of folk who make you feel comfortable and right at home from the very first "How do you do?"

David himself has a boyish countenance whose innocent look is little diminished by the small cigars he smokes habitually. The smoking, in fact, only gives him the look of a "dead-end kid" from a James Cagney film, the type of delinquent who can easily be turned from life on the tough streets through the guidance of a friendly ex-boxer turned priest.

John Hines, on the other hand, carries himself with the casual elegance of the British gentry. He wore his tweeds and cap with aplomb. Fortunately, for my sensibility, he omitted the "chops" on his cheeks.

David's parents, his sister, her fiancé, and several business associates filled out our welcoming party. All shared that unmistakably British appeal—strong sense of protocol, dry sense of humor, and high sense of culture. I could only guess at how they would perceive the Kinkade clan with our American view of things—after all, my family's idea of high culture is a pickup truck with raised suspension.

———————◇———————

David Winter's cottage was originally a mill—hence its name, Mills Cottage—and has been fashioned under David's loving care into a studio and a second home for his family. More rustic than IvyGate cottage with its lush gardens, Mills cottage does, nonetheless, have several remarkable features in its setting and architecture.

First, and perhaps the most noteworthy, the house has a river flowing through its front yard.

This is not a seasonal stream, but a full branch of the River Nore, suitable for fishing or canoeing in the summer and, from the looks of the flood plain, of careful watching in the winter. Having been raised at the confluence of three rivers, I was immediately attracted to the stream's banks and stood entranced by the gentle sounds of the water.

Certain sounds, I believe, are forever in perfect consonance with the human soul: the crash of the surf on a beach, the rustle of the wind in the trees, the babble of rushing water over rock. To live where any of these sounds could be your daily companion is restorative beyond measure. I immediately envied David Winter this beautiful riverside retreat!

Another feature of the cottage is its central fireplace. David's fireplace is big—and I say this as a resident of Texas, where *everything* is big. I would, in fact, call it the only "walk-in" fireplace I have ever seen. There is room for clothes to dry, for a pot of stew to simmer, and for wood and other fire-making necessities to be stored—all under the same chimney flue. Although this fireplace dominates the living area of the cottage, I would not call it overwhelming. It provides both a figurative and literal warmth that fits the intimate portrait of the evenings that I imagined must be spent there.

I found one of David's sculptures in progress on the table in front of the hearth, and I could envision the cold Irish night, a roaring fire, and the artist intent on his creation.

The most outstanding feature of Mills Cottage, however, is the history of the country that surrounds it. Dotted throughout the countryside that serves as the cottage's backdrop are the ruins of monasteries, churches, and castles that date back centuries. And, being the congenial hosts that they were, David and John offered a tour of a few of these local historic sites: Kilree, Kells, and Mount Juliet.

Riding with an Irish native at high speeds on the wrong side of the road is, to put it mildly, a tense experience, and John's ongoing joke that the government was "phasing in right side driving" on country roads didn't help. "The buses," he laughed, "were changed over last month, and the cars will have to meet the requirement by the end of the year." It took me a while, but I finally did appreciate why everyone else in the van was amused at my comment that the government's proposed "transition policy" was a fine idea.

Kilree, or as it might be called in English, "The King's Church," is an isolated grouping of a cemetery, the remains of a church, a watch tower, and the burial mound of the high king of ancient Ireland, Niall Caille.

The king died in a drowning accident in 844 A.D. while attempting to save a servant. So great was his heroism and sacrifice that his memorial was, for the time and culture, extremely generous and serves as a testament to his selfless act even today. The sandstone cross that marks his grave site stands nearly eleven feet tall. Gracefully carved with scenes from Scripture, this monument is equivalent in grandeur to the famed cross of Killamery.

The watch tower at this site was built primarily as a place of refuge for the abbey's monks, their manuscripts, and their sacred vessels during the occasional Viking raid. The doorway to the inside of the tower is several feet off the ground—originally an additional defense against potential invasion. Now that elevated doorway serves only as an enticement and challenge to fully grown men who believe they retain enough boyhood strength to climb it and access the inside of the tower.

Naturally I rose to the challenge by scaling the rock wall and dropping lightly into the ruin. I can only recommend you look before you leap into any dark enclosed area in Ireland. I did not, and I landed in a roost of pigeons.

I am not sure who was more startled at my abrupt entrance, myself or the birds. I can say that the birds seemed satisfied to fly to another perch and then look down their beaks on me, covered in their dust, feathers, and other leavings. I, on the other hand, was quite unhappy with their self-satisfaction. Regaining my composure and gathering what was left of my dignity, I clambered out of the tower to the cooed approval of a feathered audience.

Pigeons may be dumb birds, but I am testament to the fact that university professors can be birdbrained.

The second stop on David's and John's tour of local historical sites was the abbey of Kells, also known as Jerpoint Abbey. Known

RUINS OF ABBEY OF KELLS
IRELAND

locally as the "Seven Castles of Kells," these extensive ruins date
from 1193 A.D. Primarily built as a defensive garrison, the site
includes seven towers connected by extensive battlements and
adjoined to a large Agustian abbey. The entire complex covers fifteen
acres. At one time its aqueduct system and plumbing was fed directly
by a local river that had been diverted by medieval engineers.

I have seen many ruins in my various travels, but the Kells of
Kilkenny, without a doubt, takes the award for "Best Ruin for Playing
Hide and Seek." Everywhere you look are ingenious hiding places,
large open running lanes, and odd angled corners to peek around. I
missed my two small sons. Although Zach and Nicky are only four
and three years old (respectively), they have already discovered that
hiding from Dad is one of life's greatest joys. Their giggles make them
easy to find, but they play with an infectious fervor. What a game we
could have had in the nooks and crannies of this wonderful abbey!

I tried to interest my father in a quick game, but his knee
replacements made him much too easy to run down.

Our final stop on this whirlwind tour was the Mount Juliet golf
facility, a club and course that has been dubbed Jack Nicklaus's
favorite. A manor house and estate in the eighteenth century, the
course now boasts an international slate of professional tournaments

and a five-star hotel. As it turned out, we were to enjoy our mid-day meal there with David Winter's parents—and this company proved to be the real highlight of our visit to the country club.

Colonel Freddy, David Winter's father, who is retired from the British air force, swapped war stories with my dad, giving perspective on the "Great Conflict" from the other side of the Atlantic. The two of them seemed to have bonded to such a degree that together they were ready to storm the beaches of France again—if, as my father put it, "You would first help me out of this blasted chair!"

John Hines contributed to the entertainment with an account of the bull attack he had recently survived while enjoying a cross-country walk in England. Thom told of a similar encounter he had experienced while walking the hills that surround Norman Rockwell's studio. And I, outside of wondering if there is a bovine plot to destroy the world collectible market, got to question David's mother, Vivian, about the sculptor's childhood misadventures and notorious misbehaviors.

All and all, a very enlightening meal.

The bed and breakfast where we had reservations to stay the night was known as the Blanchville House. Its origins as a settled homestead predated the birth of the United States by at least 250 years—and may date back as far as the Norman Conquest in the early twelfth century. The Georgian manor that is currently the centerpiece of the 350-acre estate, however, was built in the 1800s to replace the original castle.

The floor plan of the house reminded me of a Southern antebellum mansion. The downstairs consists of a formal dining room, a drawing room, a kitchen, several bedrooms, and a large formal entrance dominated by a grand central staircase. Every room features high ceilings, panoramic windows, impressive fireplaces, ornate woodwork, and the Blanchville crest—an arm holding up a highly decorated sword. The current owners have decorated the house entirely in period antiques, so no sense of the present intrudes upon the house's elegant past.

As with most old British estates, the Blanchville house comes complete with "haunts." With relish, the staff and owners of the house shared two of the house's best ghost stories with me. Both of these "ghosts," I was told, belonged not to Blanchvilles but to the Kearneys, the third family to own the estate. The Kearney family held the property for more than two hundred years, up until the early twentieth century.

Blanchville House.
IRELAND

James Kearney, it seems, was an eccentric who often misspent the family fortune on whimsical personal fancy. A bell tower sits in partial ruin next to the mansion as testimony to this fact. The forty-foot tower was originally planned to stand twice its current height and to hold a clock and a full complement of bells, but was never completed. James Kearney was also an avid collector of medical texts detailing accounts of usual diseases. He was not a doctor, though; he just liked reading about disease. The remnants of his collection can still be perused in the house's drawing room.

Story has it that the spirit of James Kearney still haunts his deathbed. He apparently had a habit of scorching his whiskers with a glowing ember from the fire as a method of shaving, and this practice resulted in his burning himself to death in his master bedroom. The bed in which this tragedy occurred is still in use in the house, and, although I am not sure he knew it, Dad slept in that very bed the night of our stay. I assume that my father slept undisturbed by the ghost and that the proprietors of the house have at least flipped the mattress since James's demise.

A second tale of the supernatural details the misfortune of James's brother and his family prior to the time James inherited the estate. Although the given names of this family are lost to history, legend has it that the tragedy of their stay at Blanchville forever cursed the household.

Both James's brother and his wife of thirty-nine years died mysteriously within twelve months of each other. During this same time period, two of their three daughters also died, and the remaining child was sent to London to be raised by relatives. They say that the ghosts of the two dead Kearney children still roam the house looking for their lost sister and that no child will be safe in Blanchville house until these spirits find their peace.

Fortunately, although the night we spent there was perfect haunting weather—both windy and threatening rain—none of these lost souls chose to manifest themselves to any of our party. A few of our hosts, however, did encounter some liquid "spirits" at a friendly pub and restaurant named Langston's, where David took us all to dinner in the town of Kilkenny.

———————————◇———————————

If Ireland is the "Emerald Isle," Kilkenny is the source of much of the green radiance. So quintessentially Irish is this area that director Ron Howard chose it as the setting for the Irish segments of his movie *Far and Away.*

Langston's pub is a big part of the Irish ambiance of the area. It was originally opened several years ago by a local entrepreneur who, having once encountered success, continued to expand. Now the pub is a patchwork of connected rooms with little architectural continuity.

The menu is diverse and a wonder to the palette. I ordered salmon-stuffed mushrooms, French cheese soup, sirloin in Madagascar sauce, and Bailey's cheesecake. To be sure, a grand meal! Nonetheless, every dish that was carried past me while I waited for my own food triggered instant buyer's remorse—"Oh, I wish I'd ordered that!" Then my own meal arrived, and after the first bite I was thinking only of how to get seconds.

As at Mount Juliet, the conversation around our table proved lively and interesting. But the real memory of the evening was made not at our dinner table, but in the back room of Langston's.

While enjoying our meal at this truly Irish pub, I was surprised to hear several shouted "whoops" that sounded like they came from a Texas bull rider. I made this assessment with some authority because Fort Worth, Texas, my adopted home, boasts the "world's biggest honky-tonk," a place called Billy Bob's. This amazing establishment not only gathers several saloons and restaurants under its stadium-sized roof, but also features a concert hall, gaming areas, and a full-sized bull ring for indoor rodeos on hot Texas nights. Because I actually have eaten in a place where one can hear the sound of a Texas bull rider, I knew that sound firsthand. In any event, it intrigued Thom and me, so we went to investigate. What we discovered, as we navigated the sedate rooms of the Irish pub, was an adjoining room, filled, incongruously enough, with country western line dancers.

To my knowledge, line dancing is a trend that developed in Texas and has gained popularity in many parts of the United States. How the fad made its way to Ireland was beyond me. It is called dancing, but I, for one, am not sure that it is. For all its choreography, line dancing, for my money, is just a glorified version of the "Hokey Pokey" that we used to do at our hometown skating rink.

The odd sight of a battalion of Texas line dancers in the back room of an Irish pub was made all the odder by the fact that my brother jumped into the crowd and tried to join the line—and I followed him.

Now, it has been tradition for quite a few years that during large celebrations, such as weddings, the men in our family will get together to do what has been called the "Kinkade Strut." To gain perspective on this tradition, picture a rather bulky lifesized marionette and clone him several times over. If you were to place all of these replicants in a row and let them dance, you would have my family doing the Kinkade Strut.

The strut, however, is a simple rocking movement that all of the clan Kinkade has been able to master over our many years of practice. Line dancing, as it turned out, requires a bit more actual dancing ability. And while my brother and I are many things, we lay no claim to being dancers. I can only say that the sum total of our efforts that night made those Irish pub-crawlers look like authentic Texan-Americans—and the two of us look like authentic nuts.

To make matters worse, for one frightening moment Dad tried to join us. After jerking his replaced knees back and forth a time or two, he opted to head for the sidelines and shoot snapshots of "his boys." I'm sure they will be shown with the same pride as the photo he has of us at the age of nine and ten winning the hat dance competition in Rosarito.

———————⋄———————

Upon our return to Blanchville house, those of us who still had the energy—including Thom, Dad, and me—retired to the drawing room for some late conversation. A fire was kindled in the huge fireplace, and we all settled into the night.

I cannot, in all honesty, recount all that was said that evening. Some of the stories were so familiar that their telling became indistinct from other evenings when they were told. I will, however, make some mention of my late-night and early-morning conversation with Terry Sheppard, a video director who had been flown to Ireland by my brother's company to film the reunion between Thom and David Winter.

Terry and I fell into conversation after Thom and Dad had wandered off to bed. Like my father, Terry is a war veteran, but of a different war and with a far different view of the military experience. His perspective on life is the kind that comes only through first-hand experience with pain and trial and through his own eventual triumph over such tribulation. And his perspective on his deeply held Christian faith was one I found refreshing.

Terry wears his graying hair in a long ponytail and gives the overall impression that he would be very much at home in Haight-Ashbury during the sixties. He professes his Christianity with a distinct twinkle in his eye—a wry acknowledgment that many good churchgoers would never recognize him as one of them.

"Christ and the disciples wore their hair long," he would smile. "The radicals of their day would keep it short. Who am I to question the style of my Lord?"

The kind of "cultural Christianity" that hinges on the external trappings of religion, he might continue, serves only to divide the body of Christ and to scare away honest seekers. And it's not just a matter of appearance. How easy it becomes to squabble over our minor differences and to miss the unifying power of our common faith.

In Terry, I found a lively refutation to the belief that all Christians have to think or practice in exactly the same way. His heartfelt faith and gentle sense of humor served as a distinct comfort to me.

No one's faith should have to be lost in tangential religious arguments. To me, it is far more important to embrace the vital tenets of my faith and allow my mind to follow my spirit in its exploration.

In the end, each of us can trust God to lead us in the unraveling of life's divine mystery. That truth was as warming to me as the piping hot draft of strong Irish tea Terry and I enjoyed as we talked. Truth, in the end, is our ultimate comfort against the chill and darkness of evening.

It is as absurd to argue men,
as it is to torture them,
into believing.

CARDINAL NEWMAN
Sermon at Oxford, 11 December 1831

I V

The Sirens of Blarney

THE NEXT MORNING, as I made my way downstairs, I heard my brother talking on the phone. The tone in his voice told me that something unexpected and troublesome was happening. When I arrived at the bottom of the staircase he was just hanging up.

Thom looked up from the piece of note paper on which he was scribbling. "The ferries aren't running today. We can't get back to Wales."

"What's the problem?" I asked.

The answer Thom had gotten from the ferry company was not wholly satisfying. They had simply told him that "rough seas" had caused the cancellation. And Thom's face told me he believed that explanation about as much as I did.

It was not that we doubted the possibility that storms at sea could delay passage. It was just that the day seemed clear and mild, and I could not imagine that the water was any more unsteady than the gale-driven sea over which we had sailed to get here. There had to be something more.

Later that evening, some fellow castaways would tell us that the ferry company often canceled departures if there was not enough passenger interest to economically justify a trip. That may have been what happened. I, however, have yet another opinion. Considering the carpet and upholstery cleaning the shipping line must have had to do in the aftermath of our initial passage, they more than likely needed extra time to ready the boat for travel.

Whatever the reason, we would be stranded in Ireland for at least another day.

With a shrug of his shoulders, Thom headed off to the dining room to tell Dad of the change in plans. I joined them both and, after a sausage or two, the spirit of the journey once again took hold of us.

No boat, no problem. We would simply explore more of this beautiful Emerald Isle and discover, rather than plan, what the day would hold for us.

We loaded the car and, leaving Blanchville behind, were once again on the road. Our hosts at the bed and breakfast had suggested an interesting-sounding destination, so we were on our way to St. Patrick's Rock near Cashel in the province of Munster. And, true to Kinkade tradition, we were playing some road games to pass the time.

I am not, however, talking about "Roadside Bingo" or "I Spy." The Kinkade road games are far more interesting—although our wives might use a different word for them.

The first can be called the "I know it reads empty but I'm sure I can still get at least fifty miles out of this tank" game. The second is the "I don't know where I'm going, but I'm not going to ask because I'd rather drive in circles until I figure out this map" game. The morning we left for Cashel, I can vouch for the fact that we were playing both these manly games with gusto.

I have in my lifetime run out of gas on several occasions just because I was certain I could drive another block on what I had left in my tank. I have also spent numerous hours backtracking the miles I had driven going a wrong direction. So I am certain that had I been the driver that morning, I could have drained the tank *and* left us without transportation at some isolated point. Thom, however, was driving at the time, and he, being somewhat less adept at these games than I, actually stumbled us into a gas station after only thirty miles of idle meandering. Thom, unlike Dad or myself, seems to have lost his touch for causing true logistic catastrophe.

Since the car was being fueled anyway, we relented on our initial reluctance to receive competent direction and asked the filling station attendant how to get where we were going. As appears to be Irish tradition, however, the attendant first spent some time recounting his life story up until the point where my brother and I had entered and asked for help. He then set about commenting on the Rand McNally we had picked up to serve as our road guide.

"Ahh," he sighed while shaking his head. "This map, it'll be misleadin' ya."

"A problem?" Thom queried.

"'Tis true. This map has roads on it that naw longer exist, and is naw tellin' of others that do."

My brother and I both agreed that for a map to be so drawn would probably limit its usefulness. The commentary continued.

"You'll naw want to be usin' this. 'Tis a diabolical thing."

The idea that our misdirection was the result of a demon-infested map had not occurred to me, but the idea did not seem so far fetched. I, after all, know for a fact that there is genuine evil involved in the creation of all Christmas toy assembly instructions.

We exorcised the map by tossing it in a waste bin marked "Rubbish here, please," then followed the written directions of our "guardian attendant." An hour later found ourselves in Cashel.

The castle complex sits as guardian on top of the Rock of Cashel, a two-hundred-foot cliff jutting above the relatively flat terrain that surrounds it. It is said that this cliff, also called St. Patrick's Rock, was spat forth by Satan from the Slieve Bloom Mountains, where a gap in the limestone called the Devil's Bit fits the outcropping's dimensions. This cleft in the stone can be seen directly north of the Rock.

The castle itself was the home of the Munster kings for more than seven hundred years. And although the Arthurian legend is

Cashel Rock, Ireland

distinctly English, if there were a seat for a "round table" in Ireland, it would have to be here. Indeed, one can almost see Merlin climbing the stairs to his room in the perfectly preserved round tower for which the castle is known. The fortress structure gives an instant feel for the ancient majesty that fills Cashel's history. The structures are a hodgepodge of Irish architectural styles that reflect their construction over a period of centuries, but the overall impression is of grandeur and unity rather than confusion.

Considering the age of the complex and its importance to the historical politics of the region, it should come as no surprise that stories about the castle and its inhabitants abound. Probably the most notorious of these tales concerns the baptism of King Aengus by St. Patrick, who, of course, is credited with bringing Christianity to Ireland. Legend has it that the good saint, while performing the ceremony, pierced the king's foot with his holy staff. The king, believing that the wound he received was part of the ceremony, did not utter a protest. The cross of St. Patrick, a sculpted six-foot-tall block of stone within the fortress, serves as commemoration of this less-than-auspicious event and is said to have been the coronation site for all Munster kings thereafter.

When we arrived in Cashel, Thom, Dad, and I immediately headed for the castle to see the cross for ourselves. For my brother this visit was an effort to experience the site in an intimate way in preparation for one of his plein-air oil sketches. For my dad, who is often accused by his friends of concentrating too much on the past, the stop was yet another opportunity to learn a bit of history for "story-swapping" around the neighborhood. For me, however, the visit had a very personal overtone. On one side of this cross is a carved face of a man who is assumed to be St. Patrick—my namesake saint, as I always thought of him, his name having been chosen for me by an anonymous nun in the hospital where I was born.

My mother and father, the story goes, presumed I was going to be a girl. The expectation was so certain that they had only selected a girl's name, Nora Elizabeth, for the birth record they would be signing after my delivery. Much to my wife's eventual joy, I surprised them. The particular body parts I carried with me into the world, however, placed my parents in a quandary. What were they going to name this male child?

As my dad wandered the hospital in a daze, he happened upon a nun walking down a hall. "Hey, give me a good Irish name!" Dad blurted with customary subtlety. Without hesitation, she suggested I be named after her patron saint, Patrick. The name was immediately placed into the record on the good sister's recommendation.

This story has often saved me from the schoolyard pinches of my grammar school classmates who found me not wearing the requisite green on St. Patrick's day. Being the saint's very own namesake, I told them, set me above the tradition.

Although the story's telling generally brings a smile from my listener, when I recount the tale in the presence of my mother she can only grimace. If I am within her reach, moreover, it will gain me a punch in the arm.

Mother, it seems, rarely participated in the naming of her children. The first child, my sister, was to be named Mary Elizabeth. When my father viewed her, so the story goes, he decided she looked more like a "Katherine Henry," and he recorded her name as such without discussing the change with my mother. Mom, who along with Mother Teresa should be canonized, grinned and bore it.

My brother was always to be "William Thomas III," named after my father and grandfather, so little latitude was granted in the selection of her next child's given name. Then I came. "Little Nora" I was not, and my father's nun took the lead in the replacement name selection. My mother again lost her opportunity for any input into the process.

Although I was to be my mother's last child, life did eventually right the injustice. I am aware of at least two children she has named. She calls my first son, Zachary Thomas, "Max," and my second son, Nicholas William, "Little Ricky."

My boys always giggle at these off-the-wall nicknames, thinking their grandmother is silly or perhaps a little touched in the head. I smile, too, because I know my boys are right in both assessments. (Of course, having said so, I can also feel another punch coming.) At any rate, my connection to the good patron saint of the Emerald Isle has nothing to do with my mother!

While having my picture taken next to the cross, I was at first disappointed to discover I really bear no resemblance to the real St. Patrick. But I decided that the appearance of an eight-hundred-year-old-stone relief is probably not a desirable look for a man in his prime, so I accepted the disappointment with a minimum of chagrin.

Thom and I decided to lunch together in the village of Cashel, leaving my father to poke about the fortress and to take his time in reading all the historical information tags his heart desired. The meal was unremarkable, but I did learn two important facts about Irish cuisine.

The first is that one should avoid any food that has the word *shepherd* in its name. Those who would partake of such a dish will quickly find that the quaint and rustic image of the herdsman eating a meal of savory vegetables and meats will not be experienced through the selection. Shepherds apparently did not really eat much hearty stew. Having sampled the "Shepherd's Pie" in the local pub, I have to believe that the word *shepherd* may, in fact, translate from the Gaelic to roughly mean "one who eats things even swine would avoid."

The steaming mass of congealed food stuffs that was served to me was a gritty paste of unrecognizable meats and overcooked potatoes. It was reminiscent of haggis, a sausage pudding made of animal

byproducts and oatmeal cooked in a cow's stomach that I ate in
Scotland. All claims about the cast iron stomach of the Kinkades
aside, I would rather starve to death tending my flock then live by
eating the cuisine of shepherds.

A second thing I discovered on that particular culinary jaunt is
that any dish that has Irish cabbage as a main ingredient should be
eaten only when the period immediately following the meal can be
spent alone and preferably outside. Even the most intimate of traveling companions will appreciate the time apart, lest the romance of
the relationship be forever lost.

Much to his gratitude, after my cabbage lunch, I immediately left
Thom's company. Thom went to set up a canvas and paint while I
opted for a walk around the village.

The shops of the town offered a good opportunity for antiquing
and for examining the regional arts and crafts, and additional historic
sites were sprinkled throughout the village square area. Most
impressive of these was an old Dominican friary which, unlike the
nearby fortress, is not heavily trafficked and so offers a more relax-
ing and meditative atmosphere.

The real joy of the visit, however, came not so much from viewing the artifacts of Cashel's impressive history, but rather from taking the opportunity to meet the local townsfolk. On this particular
day I did not have to look for somebody with whom I could chat;
they were looking for me.

A group of seven children, ranging in age from toddler to young
teen, all ragged and obviously poor, found me in the ruined friary
and immediately offered their services as tour guides. For the next
hour I received a child's-eye view of Irish history and architecture.
Most of the descriptions and narratives were hopelessly fragmented
or inaccurate, but all were fun for the listen. The children seemed to
delight in my interest and my exclamations of surprise with each
"fact" they revealed. And with each look of wonderment I gave came
even greater embellishment from my young storytellers.

As I "tipped" the children for their efforts with sticks of Juicy Fruit, each offered gratitude by saying with the most profound Irish sincerity that he or she would "say a prayer for me."

———————◇———————

It was late afternoon before we were ready to leave Cashel. Thom had just finished his oil sketch, Dad had been resting in the car, and I had grabbed the moment to write a few paragraphs in my journal. A decision was quickly made to attempt to drive to Blarney Castle before heading back to the port cities and our presumed departure from Ireland the next morning.

If one looks at a map of Ireland, a quick computation will indicate that the distance between Cashel and Blarney is approximately seventy miles, certainly no more than eighty. The map will further suggest that, except for a small section heading due west out of Cork, the road between Cashel and Blarney is an uninterrupted segment of throughway number 8 out of Dublin, a major road for the isle. Traveling at fifty-five miles an hour or so, one could then expect to drive from Cashel to Blarney in about an hour and a half.

If that is your expectation, forget it.

These sorts of simple relationships between time, distance, and speed do not hold true in the real world, although for some unexplainable reason I persist in thinking they do.

My wife has traveled enough with me to ignore my estimations of time when I give them. In a typical scenario, she will ask, "How long until we get there?" I, in turn, will look at the distance, check the road type and condition, clock our speed, and give my response: "Oh, about two hours." Seven hours later we will pull over, book a motel room, and hope to get an early start in the morning to reach our eventual destination by noon the next day.

The same dynamics, predictably enough, were in place for our trip to Blarney. The road stretched or time dilated—I am not sure which—and we arrived in Blarney three hours later and an hour and a half past the official closing time of the castle and its grounds.

———————◇———————

The fame of Blarney Castle comes, in part, from the adoption of word *blarney* into the English language as a noun or verb meaning "idle flattery" or "to flatter." It is said that the expression was started by Queen Elizabeth I when Cormac McCarthy, then lord of Blarney, cajoled royal representatives into respecting his sovereign authority in the region in opposition to English rule and charter. The smooth-talking Irishman so exasperated the queen that whenever anyone used verbal subterfuge to gain advantage, she would exclaim, "That is all Blarney."

The castle also retains notoriety because of the famed "Blarney Stone" that is located in a wall of its upper battlements. Although it is difficult to reach (you must lie on your back and be lifted back and down to make the attempt), kissing the stone will supposedly guarantee those making the attempt the gift of eloquent speech and persuasiveness. Many make the trip to the castle for the sole purpose of snatching a bit of romance with this rock.

The castle is fundamentally composed of two structures, a large four-story keep and a smaller tower. Surrounding these buildings are the castle grounds, the true glory of a visit to Blarney. Flowered gardens, groves of trees, a meandering brook, and delicate rock grottos all decorate the dell in which the castle abides.

At this point, though, you may be wondering how I can personally comment on these things if, as I have mentioned, we arrived at the castle well after it had closed for the evening. In a positive light, one might simply suggest that the lock on Blarney's gated entrance did not achieve the height of technological security, and it begged a test from desperate travelers. It failed. Leaving Dad in the car to keep watch and "honk" warning, my brother and I, in true James Bond fashion, crept our way onto the castle's grounds.

This is not the first time Thom and I had participated in such shenanigans. Several times during our teens we were forced to use our ingenuity to gain entrance to a place or an event that was being denied us for what seemed, at the time at least, no legitimate reason.

In Placerville, California, the town where Thom and I spent our formative years, there was little to do during the evening. Businesses on Main Street would close, and the population of five thousand would turn toward home and family for nighttime entertainment and amusement. Only those intrepid souls who would brave the evening insects and the darkened country roads to make the trip to the out-skirts of town and the Se Rancho drive-in movie theater escaped from this routine. From childhood, Thom and I were regular escapees.

When we were small, our mother would dress us in our paja-mas and take us to the drive-in for family outings. One outstanding feature of this ritual was the "Kiddie Playland" located in a dusty field immediately in front of the drive-in screen. There we would cavort, grinding dust and dirt into our pj's until the big clock projected on the screen signaled "Showtime."

The Se Rancho of our teenage years, however, was a bit shab-bier than the one of our childhood. When we went to the drive-in, it was less to see the movie and more to see friends and be seen by others. The cost of making these appearances on a regular basis, however, was more than our limited budgets would allow, especially if we wanted to eat popcorn and hot dogs when we got inside. More often than not, therefore, Thom and I would sneak in.

Walking through the cow pastures that circled the property, stowing away in a car trunk to be let out in the back of the theater lot, lying quietly under blankets in the back of a pick-up—any method was worth trying to save the cost of admission. Usually, these meth-ods worked. If they didn't, the management would walk us out, and we would be forced to try another route of access a few minutes later.

In retrospect, of course, we can see that the family who owned the Se Rancho probably knew the routine as well as we did; they just played their part in the intrigue to prevent wholesale gate running by everyone under eighteen. Once inside—and inevitably we would make it—Thom and I would congratulate ourselves on saving the one-dollar admission and proceed to buy up all the two-dollar pop-corn and dollar-fifty soda we could carry, all the time feeling that we had really pulled one off on the management.

Other than the Se Rancho, the constant target for our stealthy entrances was our high-school swimming pool. It was not really a secret that the teenage boys in my hometown would make nightly pool visits to both cool the passions of youth and to demonstrate a mascu-line flamboyance to our peers. And it may or may not be a shock that those boys who would dare to hop the fence would also take the splash without the inconvenience of clothing. Perhaps you had to be there, but doing a cannonball in the buff to the cheers of one's friends is a truly sublime experience. Even better is reliving the episode the next morn-ing to those who were not present.

Naturally, Thom and I were fully clothed when we hopped the fence at Castle Blarney, but the feeling of exultation was similar.

Once inside the Blarney's gates, however, my apprehensions almost immediately began to eat away at my resolve in being there. Being arrested in Ireland did not seem the best adventure to report back to the friends and family waiting for my evening phone call. My brother, on the other hand, was amazingly at ease. I skirted the gar-den's edge, attempting to remain in the shadows of the trees and away from the surveillance cameras I felt would assuredly bring an armed response, while my brother nonchalantly wandered into the middle of the lawn and in front of the castle and began a sketch of its façade. I admire Thom for the passion he often exhibits for his work, but this was downright unnatural! I have to believe he truly feels that someone is watching over him because he sure does not exhibit any of my mortal concerns—like getting back out alive. So Thom sketched, I stood watch, and after about fifteen minutes we headed for the castle itself.

BLARNEY CASTLE

It was a relatively short visit, we being off the normal tour schedule, but Thom and I did manage to wander in and out of a few mysterious passageways and down through what appeared to be the castle dungeon. Then with a kiss of what we decided must be the backside of the Blarney stone, we headed back toward the main gate. At our approach, we noticed that someone was there awaiting our return. "Whoops," whispered my brother as Johnny Cash's "Folsom Prison Blues" began playing through my mind.

As it happened, our reception committee turned out to be nothing more than two scruffy backpackers who, like us, had arrived at the castle after closing. They asked how we had managed to get in. Being very obliging about such matters, we were more than happy to show them the route of our entrance as we climbed out. Waving cheerfully, they began their own explorations as we drove down the castle's entryway.

That's when the sirens went off.

Glancing in the rearview mirror, my last image of Castle Blarney was of the arrival of a security officer who, after looking though the castle's security fence, trotted back to what appeared to be a guard's quarters. Though we didn't stay to witness the arrest and probable interment in the castle dungeon, I truly hope that Thom's guardian angel decided to linger in Blarney a while longer.

There is a stone there
That whoever kisses
Oh! he never misses
To grow eloquent . . .
A clever spouter
He'll sure turn out, or
An out and outer
To be let alone.
Don't hope to hinder him
Sure he's a pilgrim
From the Blarney Stone.

FATHER PROUT
Reliques, 1860

V

A Night in Waterford, A Night in Wales

IT WAS ON THE DRIVE TO WATERFORD, where we planned to spend the night on the way back to Rosslare, that our habits of the road for this trip became truly settled. It would be late, Thom would be driving, my father would be dozing, I would be stretched out in the back of the car chattering about anything that came to mind, and we would be eating a "travel snack."

No amount of description can fully do justice to this form of repast. A travel snack, for those of you who have not put in much time on the road, is a food combination that is appealing to the palette but has no nutritive value whatsoever. It is also something that you would eat *only* under road-trip conditions.

A combination that is common to my experience of the American highway is a Hostess Ho-Ho eaten in tandem with Cheetos or perhaps a Slim Jim washed down with Butterfinger milk (a delightful concoction of milk flavored like a Butterfinger candy bar). Before you recoil, taste it; it is undeniably delicious. Inevitably, however, when you are finished eating, you will sit stunned thinking about what you have consumed.

In Britain, the concept of the road snack takes on a whole new dimension. In the United States, the two essential road-snack food groups are chips and chocolate bars. And although chocolate does seem to cross cultural and political bounds rather easily, the American-style chip does not. Americans basically eat three flavors of chip—salted chips, spiced chips, and cheese chips. The British, on the other hand, seem to enjoy deriving chip flavors from a little higher up the food chain.

For instance, we tried both "shrimp chips" and "bacon chips" and deemed them palatable road snacks. The "burger puff," however, was just too odd.

To put it simply, whereas bacon should crunch and shrimp, if deep fried, might crunch, beef should *never*, in any form, crackle in the mouth. If something crunches in your hamburger patty or your steak, the natural reaction is to startle, wondering what part of the cow might have slipped into your meal to cause that sound. The burger puff creates this effect over and over again in a relentless fashion. Eventually, the mind of the eater stops registering the puffed beef flavor and opts instead to reinvent the taste as anything but what it is actually intended to be.

The road, of course, demands that anything in the car that *can* be eaten eventually *will* be eaten to pass the time. So even the burger puffs were finished. In this case, however, the "post snack reflection time" was more traumatic than is typical.

We arrived in Waterford later than expected, and so we had to see what we could by moonlight. Although best known its for high-quality crystal, Waterford also has an interesting historic district that includes a friary, a dozen or so medieval churches, and several buildings that date to the original tenth–century Norse settlers of the region. The town also boasts a scenic harbor where, I would imagine, one could while away many peaceful hours watching the comings and goings of the fishing boats.

At the time of our arrival, however, the boats were safely docked for the night, the historic district was dark and deserted, and the glassworks and gift shops were shut up tight. Most of Waterford's delights, in other words, were overshadowed by the lateness of the hour and the prospect of a very early departure the next morning. And yet our experience of the town was nonetheless a memorable one—primarily because of our accommodation.

If you truly travel, letting each day define itself, you are likely to be forced to hole up, sleep over, or just plain survive in a variety of unusual or uncomfortable situations. My brother loves to tell of a rainy night when he and his friend James Gurney were forced to sleep next to a dumpster outside a bus station from which they had been evicted. It was raining, so they wedged the dumpster lid against the wall of the station and braced it with the dumpster itself to create a workable lean-to. Because the neighborhood was less than hospitable, they were forced to sleep in shifts. Still they managed to rest, being awakened only when the trash truck came the next morning to claim their abode.

Not to be outdone, I enjoy reliving with my wife the story of the Pines Motel, located in Washington state. This unforgettable hostelry was an unforeseen stop on our trip to Mount Rainier National Park. Our room was decorated in laminated jigsaw puzzles. Worse, the motel's beds were made of stacked mattresses without accompanying box springs, providing a swamplike body support. The experience really got out of hand, however, when the room was raided by the police at one o'clock in the morning. A fleeing felon had also selected the Pines as his refuge of choice. The only thing positive about that miserable night was the fact that it ended. In the Kinkadian worldview, fortunately, the stories resulting from such an experience made the stay worthwhile.

Our overnight stay in Waterford was going to be great story material. We took rooms in a shabby-looking establishment called The Maryland Hotel, the only place that had any rooms left at that hour of the night. After having stayed there, I can attest to the reasons behind its vacancy rate. We should have taken warning from the hotel clerk's reaction to our wake-up requests.

"We have to leave early in the morning," Thom informed her. "Can we arrange for a seven o'clock call?"

"I'm sorry," came the unhesitant reply, "no one will be here."

Visions of the hotel being abandoned through the night and of guests being unable to leave without running out on the bill swirled through my mind.

"When might we be able to be called?" Thom was standing his ground.

"Well, the cook might be in by seven–thirty or eight. . . ." The woman behind the desk made this suggestion seem normal, as if the cook frequently calls guests while scrambling eggs and preparing morning coffee.

My brother appeared unfazed by the suggestion and told the clerk the proposed arrangement would be fine.

After we had officially committed to our rooms, I encountered another oddity of the hotel. The "suite" to which I had been assigned had no entrance key—not that a key would have made much difference; the door had no lock.

"Don't worry," smiled our friendly clerk, "you'll be all right—at least for one night." I was not comforted by this. I had taken the time to glance into the pub attached to the hotel lobby and had absorbed the sight and smell of the clientele. As she waved my brother further down the hall to show him his accommodation, I began to search my quarters for a place to hide my valuables and, if necessary, myself.

"Well," I thought, "I have stayed in worse." To the Maryland's credit, the bathrooms in the hotel did not share venting. In the resort, and I use the term loosely, where we had stayed in Rosarito, the building's architect had designed just such an arrangement, allowing guests of adjoining suites to talk to each other while utilizing the facilities. Bear in mind, I'm not describing fresh air venting, but rather a port–holelike aperture which leads only to the bathroom next door. Thom and I enjoyed many pleasant conversations while otherwise fully occupied, a luxury I am convinced very few strangers would have found desirable.

To the credit of the Hotel Rosarito, the bathrooms there were actually functional. Unfortunately, the Maryland couldn't make the same claim.

Walking up the small set of stairs to the bath—I have no idea why the restroom was built four feet higher than the rest of the room—I found that my commode did not have a tank lid and that the water would not stop running through the bowl. The constant flushing sound that filled the room was bearable only by comparing it, with considerable imagination, to the soothing sound of a small waterfall. And that attempt at positive thinking was only half successful.

The problem with my father's bathroom, however, was not so easy to accommodate. My father did not fit into his shower! The walls were too close together to allow Dad to turn. He was caught in the attempt like toast in a toaster.

Now, I will fully admit that my father no longer fits into his wartime uniform, but neither is he Jabba the Hut. He should be able to fit into a shower with room to spare. Not this one. I assume that the architect who decided to elevate the bathroom in my room had a hand in the design of this shower as well.

My brother, who was spared any difficulties with the plumbing, had been given a room with a sagging mattress and no temperature control. He managed to cope with the bed by removing the mattress altogether and sleeping on the box spring, but even opening the windows had little effect on the temperature problem. The heat that began building in his room eventually became comparable to the glassmaking furnaces for which the town is famous. Fortunately, because his shower did have the capacity to hold an adult male, Thom was able to rehydrate before coming downstairs the next morning.

As planned, we did make the ferry the next day. The cook didn't even have to wake us because Dad, still a bit gamy from the lack of a shower, woke up at six and performed alarm-clock duty.

This time we would be taking the larger of the two ferries in service between Ireland and England, a massive ship the size of an oceangoing liner. The faster SeaLynx, we had been told, was still out of service for the day due to "gale force winds." With a few raised eyebrows at that assessment, we drove aboard the gently rocking ferry, whiffed appreciatively at the mild breeze, and began our slow cruise back to Wales.

Thom rented us a cabin on the ferry, and we all hit the rack to catch up on some of the sleep we had lost the previous night. Although we had not exhausted all the adventure to be found on the Emerald Isle, the Emerald Isle had truly exhausted us.

———————————◇———————————

Wales, the part of the United Kingdom to which we were returning, is truly remarkable. Within the borders of this relatively small country lie a variety of natural environments that could represent the best of many different countries. There are areas of green lushness that resemble tropical forests as well as stretches of barren, featureless wasteland that could only be called "The Great Welsh Desert." There is a spectacular coastline, easily the equal to that of Maine or northern California. And there are glaciated mountain peaks as spectacular, if not as high in elevation, as those in the Canadian Rockies.

Wales offers, in other words, just about every imaginable terrain that earth can offer—in an area you can cross in about two hours, traveling in any direction.

The most gratifying experience of Wales, however, comes through intimate contact with her people. All too often, foreign travelers assume that British culture means English culture, leaving the truly unique and grand Welsh tradition unexplored and underappreciated. But these are a people as fiercely independent as the Irish or the Scots.

Indeed, although the Welsh have been formally tied to the English since the rise of the Anglo-Norman Kings of the eleventh and twelfth centuries, the country has held tightly to its own Celtic

Village Castle, Wales

culture and language. At times during its history, the Welsh have even fought for their independence. The most notable of these wars was carried out under the leadership of Owen Glendower, a historical figure of Arthurian proportions in the Welsh mind. In the early 1400s, Owen managed to unite the Welsh people and firmly entrench the separateness they feel from their English cousins.

My brother and I had come into personal contact with the issue of Welsh independence during the night we spent in Wales before we had boarded the high-speed ferry for Ireland two days earlier. That evening we had arrived late as usual. My father was tired, so Thom and I got him settled down for the night, but then met across the street from our hotel at what appeared to be a boisterous pub.

When I entered that bustling place, I was struck immediately by three things.

First, The Red Bull, as it was called, was incredibly crowded. It was hard to imagine how such a large number of people could fit into a space that was roughly the size of a double-wide mobile home, but there they were. Moreover, they all seemed content with the complete loss of personal space.

Second, the crowd at "the Bull" was younger than we normally experienced in a British tavern. Most, if not all, of the clientele were of college age.

And, finally, my brother, even after a cursory inspection of the gathering, was not immediately apparent in the crowd. He was only a few minutes ahead of me, so I thought he would be standing off to the side someplace, perhaps studying the menu and awaiting my arrival. After two circuits through the crowd, I finally noticed Thom's familiar tweed cap at the center of a small crowd of people, all of whom were intent on a heated discussion. I was becoming somewhat perplexed over how Thom had managed to become the focal point of a group of Welsh college kids in five minutes' time, but I took a seat at the table, anyway.

At first the conversation was hard to follow. Not only were there several key participants, each offering up his or her own perspective on the topic and all at once, but there were two languages, English and Welsh, being spoken concurrently and often within the same sentence.

Welsh, as a language, is actually quite lovely to the ear but do not expect to have any understanding of it from a proficiency in English or from your high-school French, German, or Spanish. For example, the Welsh word for "Wales" is *cymru;* for "thank you," *ciolch yn far;* for "cheers," *Hwyl;* and for "hag-eyed old mouse catcher" (a common phrase of denunication), *lygodwaig hen lygadroth!*

The five hundred thousand or so native speakers of this language, besides using it for odd insults, also speak it to isolate and insulate themselves from the English. This application of the ancient Celtic tongue is apparently especially pronounced among the young Welsh, who feel their lack of social and economic potential is a result of an exploitative tie to the rest of Britain.

The discussion developing this night was primarily political in nature. The group was elaborating on the divisions that exist within the Welsh populace. Deannes, a young dark-haired student from a local university, was insisting that deep cultural differences existed between the Welsh who live in the north and those who reside in the south. I could relate. Growing up in Northern California, I constantly heard all about the superficial, smog-dazed Los Angelenos. Then while in college in Southern California, I heard about the snobbish, tree-hugging San Franciscans.

Gyen, another college student, offered the perspective that the greatest divisions in Wales were between the generations. She felt close ties to her grandparents but was alienated from her parents. The current economy of Wales, she continued, offered little hope to the generation beginning their careers in the 1990s. Her grandparents understood her need to break from the Welsh culture to find success in the world, but her parents only pressured her to find her future at home.

I smiled at the sincerity of Gyen's descriptions and her assumption that she was alone in this outlook. As a university professor, I have heard this many times from my American students. I spoke of these things myself when I was a student, and I can remember my older sister, Kate, feeling the same in her time. The angst involved with breaking away from home and entering adulthood is timeless, universal, and, once you move beyond its turmoil, sweetly nostalgic.

After these observations regarding the state of Wales, the conversation drifted to the Welsh students' feelings toward the British. And had the fight and eventual street riot not broke out, I am sure the evening would have ended with a recap of the Welsh desire for independence.

The altercation that erupted was between two young men over, as I suppose tradition would dictate, the affections of a young woman. Once the battle lines were drawn, several others in the pub immediately involved themselves but, fortunately, only by speaking in rather excited Welsh. Individual tempers flared, but the cooler heads prevailed, and the combatants were restrained by their respective camps.

The only major casualty of this initial confrontation was my shirt. In the first moments of the row, one of the instigators was thrown into my table, and ale went everywhere—mostly on me. My brother remained strangely untouched by the dousing (which was fortunate, since he was working on a sketch of a Welsh dirt farmer sitting at our table, known, oddly enough, as Skipper). Feeling that discretion

"SKIPPER"
WELSH DIRT
FARMER

"I ALWAYS
WORKED WITH
ME BACK AND
HANDS.."

was the better part of valor, I held back any sort of protest about the results of the scuffle and simply moved out of harm's way to watch the event unfold.

I sincerely believe things would have settled at this point had no one else attempted to interfere. The unfortunate reality, though, was that further intervention turned a simple ruckus into disaster.

On the occasions when a boyhood argument would break out between Thom and me, the single worse strategy my mother could take would be to directly impose herself into the circumstance. Mom's presence in our disagreements, more often than not, only encouraged Thom and I to rally against her imposed authority. At such times, Mom's only recourse was to bring out her ultimate weapon: The Mop. This article commonly lay dormant in the corner of our bathroom, but when seen in Mom's agitated grasp, our boyhood hearts trembled with fear. Though we knew Mom would never actually strike us with The Mop, we were convinced that coming within three feet of its ratted end would immediately infect us with an incurable disease. Its effect was indeed calming.

Thom and I rallying together against Mom highlights a simple dynamic: Brothers stand up for each other. If I want to gut punch my brother, it's okay; if anyone else tries, he would have had a reckoning with me. Thom is my brother, and only *I* can punch him. I know, without asking, that Thom loves me in the same violent way. And I believe a similar dynamic was at work when the English police arrived to break up the fight at the Red Bull—the Welsh students saw themselves as a brotherhood united against the English.

By the time the officers arrived, the crowd had unified around a single thought—that these outsiders were interfering in family business. As the pub emptied out onto the street, the crowd was speaking almost exclusively in Welsh. The English officers seemed fully intent on crowd control; they were attempting to detain and question the two principles in the pub fight. The crowd, on the other hand, seemed to focus the whole of their political outrage on these accessible symbols of English rule. Shouting and insults escalated. For a time it seemed a Welsh chant of solidarity emerged from the crowd, but this was soon drowned by the general noise. Out of the corner of my eye a surreal vision caught my attention. Two drunk boys, one of which sported a top hat for no apparent reason, had constructed a small bonfire from newspapers which was burning festively atop a barroom chair that had been dragged into the alley. In a consumate act of

COLLEGE STUDENT
WITH TOPHAT
WALES

artistic chutzpah, Thom had positioned himself beside the boys and was busily sketching by the light of the fire. "Nice effect of light on the guy with the top hat," Thom later told me.

Suddenly, an object sailed over the heads of the crowd. I could see it was an empty beer bottle, and I jumped to avoid it as it crashed hollowly on the ground beside the police officers. More shouts, then a muffled comment followed by peels of laughter from the crowd. The situation was tense. Student protest may seem safe or even a bit romantic when viewed from an armchair or through the pages of your favorite news magazine, but the personal experience of it can be downright frightening.

The situation resolved itself when, to the cheers and jeers of the crowd, the two central players felt the need to empty their stomachs on the sidewalk in unison. It was not difficult for the police to take the two into custody at this moment of vulnerability. The officers then quickly exited from the scene, leaving the crowd to disperse back into

the pub or other eating and drinking establishments along the boule-
vard.

Thom and I found each other on the street; we had both lost track
of the group with which we had been talking.

"A little bit rough," offered my brother as he approached. The
statement, an old inside joke that is too "inside" to even begin to
explain, drew a smile from me.

"Wow! Bang! Schwack!" came my obligatory response. What
else could be said?

I was reliving this adventure from a day or two earlier in a semi-
dreamlike aboard the ferry state when I heard Dad's voice, "Son, get
up! I'm hungry. Let's get some breakfast." I groaned at yet another
awakening, this time on the ferry returning to Wales. My dad was
rapidly becoming Father Time's evil twin, Padre Alarm Clock.

mi ddawnsiaf y Gymru Rydd
Mi ganaf gan y Gymru Rydd
Ac rwy'n yfed i doriad yr hyfryd ddydd
Y dydd y bydd pob Cymro'n rhydd!

I'll dance the dance of Wales Free
I'll sing the song of Wales Free
And I drink to the dawn of the lovely day
The day when every Welshman will be Free!

DAFYDD IWAN
Bod Yn Rhydd

V I

Woodland Walks

AFTER DOWNING an overly large, greasy, bland, but otherwise quite pleasant brunch, we returned to our cabin aboard the ferry to England and attempted to catch up on sleep. By the time we drove onto the docks at Fishguard it was noon, and we felt refreshed. We headed east toward London.

The weather that morning was cool and partially overcast. The clouds caused the sunlight to pillar towards the earth and splash in patches on the ground. It was a beautiful effect, and seeing that my brother's gaze was beginning to linger more on the scenery around us than on the road in front of him, it was obvious what was coming.

"Pat, is there anything of interest close up ahead?" Thom asked.

"Nothing on the map," I answered, fumbling through the various guides and travel books strewn about the car.

"I think I see an exit," he said. "Let's check it out. I might find a subject. This light is fantastic, and I don't want to waste the opportunity to capture it. Artist rule number one, 'Never pass up an inspiration in the hopes of finding something better.'"

"Seize the moment," I capitulated, quoting my favorite "dead poet," Alexander Pope.

We turned off the main road and drove up into rolling Welsh hills. Ignoring the signs pointing the way to Gelli or Bethesda, we instead followed a set of historic markers that guided us toward a township called Parish Llawhaden. Although the name, like every other Welsh word, was nearly impossible to pronounce, I found later that it has a relatively simple meaning. Llawhaden translates roughly as "The Land of Aidan." Aidan was the patron saint of a historically important church in the parish and a follower of St. David, the patron of Wales.

As we entered the town, it did not take long for my brother's subject or his artist's perspective on it to make itself apparent. Llawhaden not only boasts a significant church, but the township also has its own fortress. The ruin of Castle Llawhaden is peacefully situated against the pastoral Welsh countryside. My brother was immediately entranced.

"Do you think you guys can find something to keep yourselves occupied for awhile?" Thom smiled. "I love this place."

———————————◇———————————

Leaving my brother happily painting the castle and my father reading a book describing the battlefields of World War II, I set about discovering what else the area might have to offer. My first thought was to visit a small retirement home I had noticed a mile or so down the road from the castle view where we had stopped. I always look at such a residence as a rich storehouse of oral history and social insight. If one wants to truly get to know a culture, I am convinced, one of the best things to do is spend time with its elderly.

Unfortunately, the management of the home had strict policies about visitors. As I walked back down the pathway to the road, I waved through the wrought-iron fence to the folks on the other side. Several smiled and waved back. This was, without a doubt, a lost opportunity for those on both sides of the fence.

———————————◇———————————

I decided to take a walk in the countryside, even though the earlier promise of a mild day had evaporated. A cold overcast had settled onto the parish, and now the clouds were beginning to darken and lower themselves into a thick, patchy fog. A person disappears into it, only to reappear suddenly further down the trail before vanishing again. The wind at this point had also picked up to a lonesome howl.

In such an atmosphere, I could easily imagine the "fairy folk" or the "others" (as the locals call them) that inhabit much of the rich Welsh folklore. Superstitions are created on days such as these and in places such as Llawhaden. In the back of my mind, as I walked through the magical, somehow ominous mist, I could almost hear the townsfolk warning, "Stay off the moors. Stay off the moors!" as if I, an outsider, might meet the mischief or wrath of the "others" if I were to venture too far afield. I was thoroughly enjoying the feeling.

A sign in Llawhaden suggested that if I walked a bit farther I could intercept a wayfaring trail between Gelli and Conaston Bridge that would take me along the East Cleddau river. The sign also promised that if I were to keep a keen eye on my surroundings I might be able to spot a salmon or brown trout in the river, a specklewood butter-fly or a kingfisher in the air about me, or an otter playing among the cowslips, foxgloves, and bluebells at the river's edge.

I am not enough of a naturalist to know my cowslips from my foxgloves, but I do recognize that when I isolate myself from every-day cares and open my senses to the world around me, a walk in the woods will renew my spirit and mind in ways beyond simple rest and relaxation. The mystics of Nepal and India regularly refind them-selves on such "treks"; the aborigines in Australia use the "walkabout" in the same manner; and the American backpacker, whether on the Pacific Crest, the Continental Divide, or Appalachian Trial, knows well the peace that can be found while hiking through God's creation.

So I decided to take the trail. I had no particular destination in mind except within myself and had no particular purpose in the walk but to open my eyes and experience the natural world firsthand. But who knew, in this place where enchanted kingdoms seemed so near, what else I might encounter on the way?

I had been on the trail for just less than an hour but had already grown used to hearing nothing but the wind and the sound of my own footsteps. The only hint of civilization nearby was in the faint smell of chimney smoke that the now cold air reluctantly revealed. The powerful image of warm hearths that the smell brought to mind worked in stark contrast to the overwhelming feeling of isolation that the countryside provided.

It was at this time, when the solitude was just beginning to work within me, that a stranger intruded upon my ramble. I never heard his approach, and I only became aware of my new traveling companion when he began licking my hand.

Recovering from my surprise, I found myself walking beside a small black-and-white terrier that bore a striking resemblance to the first dog that I can remember having as a pet. Thom and I had called our dog Tipper, and so I used that name to refer to my newfound friend. Watching his jaunty, confident walk, I found myself reminiscing about the days when Tipper was part of our lives.

That little dog was far from the only pet my brother and I adopted in our boyhood. To list just a few, we had dogs named Shag-Rug, Sambo, and Gollybird; cats named Bunny, Guy, and Bates Floater; and a goat named Nanny. In fact, there was a time in our rural childhood when we owned twenty-four cats and thirteen dogs at once. But Tipper was something special. He was by far the smartest dog I have ever known, and although we claimed him as our pet, we were never quite sure that he fully claimed us.

Everybody knew Tipper; he was a dog about town. He had no master but used various people to his own end and related to people only as he saw fit. He was a bit like the dog Tramp in the classic Disney cartoon, *Lady and the Tramp*, except our Tipper was less of a scoundrel and more of a prince—graciously condescending to be fed and patted as he trotted confidently from house to store to flower shop.

Although it was nice to imagine that my old friend Tip had somehow come back to walk the trail with me, this latter-day impostor turned out to have much less personality than his earlier counterpart. He did, however, have Tipper's keen sense of smell. Nuzzling against my jacket pocket, he directed me to the last of the burger puffs that remained from the night before. These I happily shared, hoping that the dog's enjoyment of this snack food did not reflect an overly hasty reading of its package label. "Burger puff" and "puppy puff," after all, might be easy to confuse.

———————⟡———————

I was about ready to turn back from my trek when I came across another bit of any country childhood—a rope swing, swaying gently in the wind under a substantial oak tree.

There is not a summer I can remember that did not include building or playing on some kind of rope swing. When we were younger such swings were small and tame; they simply dangled from an overhanging limb in the yard and invited us to swing in gentle arcs. As we grew, however, so did our swings; the ropes became stouter and the trees became taller, and we sought out higher and riskier opportunities to soar.

The pinnacle of our swinging experience probably came in our late teen years with the "diamond dam" rope. This particular swing was hung from a tree that overlooked a cliff above the water of an old reservoir. The hearty soul that attempted this fabled swing would have to garner the courage to hold to this rope as it moved in a great landbound arc, releasing his grip just in time to be thrown out over the cliff and into the water. The total drop from the combination of the swing and the cliff could be measured in several full seconds and beats of the heart.

Kids from miles around would drive to that swing to test themselves and watch others be tested. Amazingly, none who made the journey ever returned worse for the effort. It must be true, as E. B. White put it, that "children almost always hang onto things tighter than their parents think they will."

Although I think it is true that most children will hang on tighter than a mother would think possible, at the same time, there are some children who will attempt to take a swing farther and faster than ever before. Occasionally and inevitably, one will take a fall. My brother was one of those kids. There were three or four years of his preteen life that Thom seemed always on the mend from a injury obtained as a result of attempting some new rope swing record.

My mother had fiery red hair before this period in my brother's life. After that, she lost that red to gray. It might also be said that justice is eventually served in this life. The wheel of time is turning, our children are growing, and I noticed a large tree with strong limbs that overhangs a small stream behind Thom's studio IvyGate Cottage. Thom's hair, I've noticed, has one or two gray hairs beginning to emerge.

The swing I had happened upon on that Welsh trail was much less formidable than many of those from my youth. But as time would have it and as I am pained to admit, I am much less formidable than I was in my youth.

It was a respectable swing and had a sound feel to it. It was something my adult body and perspective could still attempt—and so I did.

The ride was as I remembered.

———————◇———————

When I returned from my walk, I found my brother had finished his oil sketch and had found an open tower in the Castle Llawhaden in which to sit and share some time with my father. The view from this vantage point was spectacular—a slowly descending valley shrouded with the delicate Welsh mist and the wind rushing through the grasses, flowers, and trees.

The scene was both commanding and intimate, perfect for reminiscence.

My brother chewed the end of his unlit pipe. I sipped some cider I had brought from the car. My dad talked. We listened.

———————◇———————

In the fall of 1942, my father was working as a manual laborer in the service of the Civilian Conservation Corps, cutting timber and clearing land. The war in Europe was fully engaged, Japan had bombed Pearl Harbor, and many of America's finest young men had already followed their sense of patriotism into battle. It was at this time that Dad and a friend from the Corps made the decision to join the military and do their own part "for God and country." Dreams of adventure, a sense of duty, and the naiveté of youth swam in their heads and dictated their resolve. Abandoning their jobs, they gathered their belongings and headed for Coffeeville, Kansas, the local recruitment center.

Thrown together with thousands of other recruits in basic training, my father had the good fortune of falling under the influence of the "Crescent City Flash," a self-styled lady's man from Louisiana who was the staff sergeant in charge. "Crescent," at the time Dad met him, was primarily concentrating his considerable talents into two pursuits outside of feminine conquest.

The first of these was to get out of the army. An army regular for many years prior to the war, Crescent had decided he had been through enough. In the year prior to making my father's acquaintance, he had begun a letter-writing campaign to President Roosevelt asking for release from his enlistment. It is unclear why the President responded to these requests by putting him in charge of basic training, but that is what happened, and that is how Dad became his protégé.

Crescent's other pursuit was aimed at developing angles to get around his superiors and make military existence more bearable. His teachings were many but can best be summarized by his successful demonstration of how one could get through morning inspection by the base captain in one's underwear. Boots, leggings,

United-States-Army-issue boxer shorts, and a long raincoat to use as cover were all that were needed. As my dad describes it, he and his mentor spent most of basic training wearing very little but a trench coat. (With that in mind, the nickname "Flash" takes on new and appropriate meaning.)

After my father graduated basic and left the influence of the Crescent City Flash, he spent the next several months bouncing to and from a variety of specialized schools and training programs. In the time before he was sent overseas, Dad was trained as a dorsal gunner, a jackhammer operator, an airplane-packaging specialist, and a driver for a half-track personnel carrier. My father is not sure why the army gave him this particular combination of skills, but after he had them, his command deemed him fully "combat ready" and shipped him out. The H.M.S. Trumpeter, a British aircraft carrier with a cracked hull, provided his passage to England from Staten Island, New York. The fact that the ship's bilge pumps were already operating furiously as the vessel moved out of the harbor seemed a bad omen to Dad, but he assumed the British Navy knew what they were doing.

This initial passage lasted fourteen days and, to hear Dad tell it, the voyage was rough, unsettling, and bordering on madness. His confidence in the British Navy fell off considerably after a few days at sea. The ocean swells of a north Atlantic winter may reach thirty feet and can pitch a ship, even one the size of an aircraft carrier, so severely that on an uphill wave trough, you had to balance yourself on all fours to be able to walk. Dad insists that at times the up-and-down motion was so intense that the ship's props would be pulled out of the water and would spin freely in the air a moment before being plunged back into the water at the bottom of a trough. The sea, in fact, claimed several unfortunates on that trip who lost their balance during particularly jolting rolls and fell overboard. Despite the shouts and cries from these pitiful souls, the ship moved on to its destination. This was wartime, after all, and schedules had to be kept.

Motion sickness, as one might guess, was the norm. Some of the soldiers on the passage were so debilitated that they were unable to leave their bunks for the entirety of the voyage. And, to make a bad situation nearly unbearable, the British provided a bill of fare to the queasy recruits that included "fish and bean" breakfasts, a gamy "lamb stew" for dinner, and a wee "snort" of bad rum to wash down either meal. If the rocking did not do in your stomach's resolve, meal call would. Fortunately, Dad is blessed with a cast-iron stomach (like his sons). He not only managed to survive the shipboard cuisine but also routinely helped his companions clear their plates. Nevertheless, by the end of this passage, the European theater of combat was beginning to seem an infinitely more desirable alternative to life aboard ship.

My father landed in Boothe, England, and was to be sent by train to Bishop's Stortford outside of London in preparation for his eventual deployment to France. He was twenty-four and by the time of his arrival had risen in rank to line corporal. "Two O'Clock Jump" and "Brazil" were the radio hits of the moment, Humphrey Bogart and Betty Grable were everyone's favorite Hollywood stars, and *Gone with the Wind* had just hit the bookstands.

That was December 1943, the month when my dad began his personal invasion of Europe.

"Those were good years, Son." Dad was looking out at the lush valley. His eyes seemed full of the soft Welsh mist.

———◇———

It was late, and we still had many miles to drive before we would arrive in London. We began the climb down out of our tower.

In all the time we had spent at the old fortress, we had not seen another visitor, and we had gradually came to think of it as "our" castle. This perception, however, changed when we reached the central courtyard. At the base of the tower stairs, we met the true proprietress of Llawhaden, a young woman named Jen.

Although it was her mother-in-law who held the official governmental position of "castle keep," Jen had for years used the site for personal reflection and, as only the British could phrase it, to "catch a sneaky fag" (have a cigarette). She delighted in the fact that we were using the castle for quiet conversation and that we had a curiosity about its history. When asked, Jen told us the story of Llawhaden.

The area had been inhabited since the twelfth century B.C, but the current township was not established until medieval times. With the construction of Castle Llawhaden came a marketplace and a permanent population under Norman rule. Although Henry VIII had most of the castle destroyed in the sixteenth century, the site remained a local economic center.

Legend has it that the lands on which the castle was built originally had to be won from Satan in a barrel-rolling contest. In this event the contestants had to race each other down a hill rolling inside a barrel. Archbishop Bernard, an eighth-century clergyman, had the honor of contesting the devil, and he won. When Satan lost, he turned into a snake and abandoned all claim to the area, leaving it to the intrepid archbishop for his ministry. More recently, Graham Sutherland, a noted British artist, used the area a source of inspiration for a series of paintings. The artist, Jen said, apparently loved the mists and the primroses that are so common about the Llawhaden countryside. Jen also noted that over five hundred varieties of primroses grew on the castle grounds. Having grown up in the arid Sierra foothills we were impressed.

Poison oak was more common than wildflowers where we were raised, and the splashes of color we saw as a result were more from skin rashes than dew-soaked petals. The Sierras did, however, provide Thom and I the opportunity to engage in "rolling contests" of our own. Of course, we used tires (not barrels), and when we climbed inside and started down our hometown hills, we anticipated rolling through 500 different varieties of snakes (as opposed to primroses). In retrospect, I am convinced the Bishop had far less to fear from Satan than we had from some aspects of our boyhood "fun".

Bloomsbury Café

As the hour grew late, we left Jen to her castle and once again returned to the open road. Even her kind nature and gentle wit had not stifled the lure of what might lie up ahead.

Our arrival in London later that night was preceded by an extreme and unexplainable desire for Chinese food. When in London and when experiencing this type of craving, there is but one district to visit: Soho. This area has been called a street circus. But Soho might also be thought of as an urban jungle, in which case I was about to take my second walk of the day through the woods.

An area of rich history, London's Soho has served as home for such literary luminaries as Daniel Defoe, William Blake, and Thomas De Quincey. Karl Marx wrote *Das Kapital* in a small flat overlooking Dean Street. Once noted for its French and Italian restaurants, Soho has in recent years undergone dramatic changes in its character. The southern part of the district has been steadily encroached upon by London's Chinatown, while the rest of the area has been degraded by bawdy discotheques and assorted "Gentlemen's Clubs."

Most highly cosmopolitan cities have districts like this. San Francisco has the Broadway Strip, New York has Times Square, and New Orleans has Bourbon Street. Walking through these areas one sees an odd mix of humanity, from the conventioneer to the con man, from performance artist to the panhandler.

The burlesque "barkers" who are a regular feature of any of these areas have always held a personal fascination for me. Although they are generally the most unseemly of people, barkers have been hired to work as the sales point for the so-called "attractions" that lie hidden behind the entrance curtain. I would think that someone appealing or at least clean would be used as a front to bring in the customer, but this is almost never the case. The typical barker looks like someone who lost his job as a "carney" because of poor hygiene or lack of professional standards.

Striking up a conversation with these particular denizens is not a problem, and a passerby who is willing to listen through their "pitch" will find that many have interesting experiences to relate. To me, it is a lot like dealing with certain sales representatives. You have to have patience to get to the good stuff.

While in New Orleans many years ago, I befriended "Brother Jim," a barker who bore an uncanny resemblance to Henry, a college friend with whom I was traveling. In all fairness—and so Henry will remain my friend after reading this—I should specify that the resemblance was limited to facial features only, for Jim was unshaved, unshowered, and unsavory, to say the least. And he wore really bad suits. (All right, the resemblance to Henry involved a little more than the face.)

Henry and I introduced ourselves to Jim by asking a question we had standardized into one of our travel routines: "Where's the party?"

Surprisingly, most people would attempt a response to this question, as though the entire metropolis was coordinating a city-wide celebration. Not surprisingly, specifics at a certain point became vague—and this was certainly true in the case of brother Jim. He really had no idea where the party was or why we were asking him about it. He did, however, like to talk, and we eventually took him out for a late night cup of coffee.

It turned out that Brother Jim had lived many years as a Benedictine monk but had left the order because of personal uncertainties about his beliefs—and certain improprieties involving various members of the community. His appearance to the contrary, Jim was an intelligent and sensitive individual who had an interesting perspective on life and the universal order of things—one that could only come from the rather unusual blending of his monastic life and his "barker" experiences.

In Soho, Thom, Dad, and I walked about for some time, watching people and, in turn, being watched. We talked to a few of the apparent regulars of the district, but found no "Brother Jim" to offer us a late-night diversion. We did find, however, that we had lost our interest in Chinese food and so decided to call it night. After checking into our hotel and going upstairs to unpack, Thom and I planned to meet in the hotel sitting area for a light snack.

It was while enjoying our tuna sandwiches that we met Neil, the night manager of the hotel, an energetic Welshman who claimed to be "a millionaire in training"—what others call, ironically enough, a sales representative. After working through his pitch, he told us great stories of his time in the British military and his wartime recollections of the Falkland Island conflict in 1982.

Unfortunately, our night manager had no better information on where "the party" was than Brother Jim did, but I still had to ask.

"The party?" Thom asked skeptically. "Will there be balloons?" I assured him that no celebration would be complete without them.

It was getting late. I didn't find the elusive party that night, though I'm sure someday I will.

If not, who knows? Maybe *I'll* throw it.

Enter these enchanted woods,
you who dare.

GEORGE MEREDITH
The Woods of Westermain

VII

London for the Eccentric

KINKADE TRAVEL PRINCIPLE NUMBER ONE:
The offbeat is often better than the tried-and-true. I demonstrated this travel principle to my wife several years ago when we were visiting Rio de Janeiro. Although at first apprehensive about my forays off the beaten path, Laura now fully admits that the most memorable moments of this trip were theones we spent away from the crowds an din search of the unique. We did make the obligatory trip up to Sugar Loaf Mountain, but we also visited the obscure but delightful Carmen Miranda Museum (a tribute to a "celebrity" that Laura knew only as the Chiquita Banana lady). We also attended (with the help of a local) a ritual dance at a house of "worship" for the local pantheistic form of religion. The ritual involved lots of flailing arms and various types of poultry. Between the smoke and the chickens, I thought I had lost Laura's confidence a couple of times, but upon reflection we both recognized it as an exceptional cross-cultural experience.

If you are in London for the first time, then by all means visit Buckingham Palace and see the Changing of the Guard. But along these travel staples, try to wander just a bit off the beaten path—you'll thank me for the advice.

I arose very early in the morning. This was going to be our only day in London, and I did not want to waste a moment.

Now, I am normally a night person, and the infrequent times that I have seen the daybreak have usually occurred when I was just returning home after a late-night work session or one of those endless caffeine-fueled discussions of the mysteries of the universe usually staged at the local Denny's. So rising with the sun was a rare occasion for me, and this made it seem all the more special. From the golden light that surrounded me as I walked out into the freshly washed English air, I knew it was going to be a beautiful day.

We had stayed in the Hotel Rubens, which is virtually next door to Buckingham palace. I have visited London on several occasions and had seen the palace many times, but this morning was different. The crowds had not yet arrived, and I could actually just sit for a moment and take in an unobscured and uninterrupted view of the whole building.

I might have lingered in the front of the palace, sitting quietly at the Queen Victoria Memorial to watch the early-arriving crowds, but I had another idea. It occurred to me that attempting to annoy an English palace guard has become a tradition for any American visitor to London. Everyone, it seemed to me, makes an attempt to force the black-hatted guards out of their rigid stance of attention and get them to crack a smile. I, however, was more interested in actually talking to a guard about his experience of the visitors who make this effort. My thought was to walk along St. James's Park, down Birdcage Walk, and toward the Wellington Barracks and the Guards Museum in the hopes of meeting some of the Queen's Bivouac off duty and open to conversation.

I made it about a hundred yards down the street when I heard them coming. The sound of a military unit approaching double-time is unmistakable, especially when they are engaged in the standard running chants. Although, unlike their American counterparts, the British Army apparently doesn't make a practice of questioning the sexual desires of the British Navy in their cadence calls, they did chant several interesting observations about their own prowess in this regard.

It did not take long for them to pass me, and they stopped only a half-block further down the road. I hurried after them as they were dispersing into a gated compound, hoping to find someone to talk to me. As fortune would have it, two were left carrying on a conversation between themselves, making them an easy target for my approach.

My tack was simple. I told them I was a university professor writing a book about the English and their perspectives on Americans and wondered if they could spare a moment to talk with me. In other words, as out of character as this is for me on this sort of venture, I approximated the truth! Sean and Alex, as they introduced themselves, were mildly perplexed by my request but, apparently judging me as harmless, indulged my interest.

For those of you who are curious, the British Guardsmen know they look like incredibly large Q-tips, and they have also heard the suggestion about "getting a haircut" many times over. And, yes, they insist, anything we may have heard about men with big hats is true. Furthermore, although they really cannot allow anyone to knock on their chests or heads to ask if anyone is home, they do appreciate the occasional young ladies "flashing." To this, however, they cannot respond appropriately until "off-posting."

———————————◇———————————

As my guardsmen left to return to their responsibilities, I continued my wanderings toward Big Ben and Whitehall Street. By doing this, I was making my way past 10 Downing Street toward Trafalgar Square and Charing Cross Road.

Trafalgar is the oldest public square in the city of London and, as such, has long been a gathering place for the city's population. Whether because of a political rally or a New Year's revel, a milling crowd can always be expected, and this makes the square an excellent spot for people watching. Trafalgar Square is also the site of Nelson's Column, an impressive commemoration of Admiral Horatio Nelson's victory over Napoleon's navy off the coast of Trafalgar in Spain. The victory, often cited as the most important moment in British naval history, was won at the cost of Lord Nelson's life. The memorial is respectfully guarded for all time by four immense bronze lions.

To my mind, however, neither the people nor the column are the true stars of Trafalgar Square. The main attraction is the birds, especially the pigeons. Fat and unafraid, they gather there in great numbers, attracted by the people who buy seeds from vendors and feed them.

It was here, among this multicolored flock, that I hoped to experience something I have wondered about since childhood.

In my youth, you see, I must have seen the Alfred Hitchcock film classic *The Birds* at least five times, and its viewing left me with two enduring theories.

The first was that with a good motorcycle helmet and a Louisville Slugger, I could survive the most cataclysmic attacks on humanity that Hollywood can envision. After all, how tough could a flock of pigeons be?

The second theory was that, except when they are pecking out your eyes, being flocked by a bunch of birds might be rather fun.

Attempting to test my first theory probably would have landed me in jail; I have no doubt that British authorities would frown on any form of birdball. The pigeons of Trafalgar Square did, however, allow me to test my second assumption. I layed on the pavement, covered myself with a "suit of seed," and was soon swarmed. The birds landed about my shoulders and head and, as I sat, they nibbled everywhere there was seed to be had.

I can truthfully say that being a dinner table for a flock of birds is amusing both for the human bird feeder and for any gathered onlookers. As with any circumstance involving a hearty feeding of birds, I do recommend shower caps be worn at all times by spectators.

Charing Cross Road, my next stop, runs off of Trafalgar Square in roughly a northeasterly direction. The street is the site of the last of the twelve "Eleanor Crosses" erected to commemorate the burial journey of Eleanor of Castile, the wife of Edward I. Edward, who ruled in the thirteenth century A.D., had a stone cross built to designate each spot where this funeral procession stopped between Nottinghamshire, where his beloved wife had died, and London, where she was buried in Westminster Abbey.

More recently, the street was immortalized in Helene Hanff's wonderful book, *84 Charing Cross Road* (followed by a play and

PAT FEEDING BIRDS, LONDON

movie by the same name), which described the one-time slum area as being a haven for used book stores. This description of Charing Cross Road is still largely accurate and was the reason for my walk in its direction.

I have always been a book person and come from a family of like thinkers. I am not sure where the fascination comes from, but somewhere between my mother's voracious reading and my sister's work at the county library, Thom and I both were instilled with a deep and abiding appreciation for the written word. To this day my mother has an entire room in her bungalow devoted to her book collection. My sister Kate's collection of mysteries and assorted novels flows through every room in her home, and Thom's collection of monographs on obscure artists numbers into the thousands of volumes and should probably make its way into a museum someday. It was my fascination with books that led me to believe there is no better place to discover odds and ends about the areas you might be visiting than in local, independent, and preferably secondhand bookstores. The reasons for this are relatively simple.

First, the people who frequent or run such establishments are by nature readers, which means they will often know the history of an area better than any other single source of information you might come across. Their interests, moreover, are likely to be both wide and offbeat, so they may well be a gold mine of unusual facts.

Second, this particular group of people, more than any other (besides, perhaps, barbers), loves to chat. This common trait in book people probably results from the fact that half of the joy of learning something new is sharing what you have learned with someone else.

Third, independent bookstores are more likely to carry the self-published texts written by local authors on topics of such restricted interest or questionable source that no major publishing house would accept nor chain store sell it. Some of these books are horribly written and offer only a rambling and completely unsubstantiated narrative. Others, however, are truly delightful and will give the traveler unparalleled access to a local sense of place, event, or historical circumstance.

One such work I found in my travels concerned the communes that existed and still exist along the Pacific Coast Highway in California. During the 1960s, the coastal mountains of California stretching between Hearst Castle in the south and Big Sur in the north became a Mecca for the counterculture. Young idealists in search of a utopian existence flocked to this area and set up small, self-governing retreats from society at large. Traveling up this stretch of road one summer in the seventies, I happened upon a small gallery that sold a diary about these communities and a guide to their whereabouts. It was a joy to read and opened up many points of reference to use in conversation with the locals.

A final thought about the utility of the used book store to the traveler—I find that there is no better place to buy a memento. A book by an author associated with an area is an excellent choice of souvenir. A book by an author associated with the area who also holds personal significance is even better. I treasure my copy of Robert Louis Stevenson's *Doctor Jekyll and Mister Hyde*, purchased from a store in Edinburgh just a few blocks from the pub where he wrote it, and my copy of Henry David Thoreau's *Walden* bought in a small town a few miles away from that famous pond.

And for my tastes, the older the book, the more desirable the purchase. Old books seem to tell a story greater then the author's printed words. These volumes have personal histories and past owners that can be sensed from the wear on the cover or read from the inscriptions on the bookplates inside. Trust me, not even a cast sculpting of Big Ben or a pillow with a likeness of the queen can offer as much as a book by one of the English literary greats, purchased from a dusty old bookshop on Charing Cross Road.

I took from my excursion on Charing Cross two first editions from P.L. Travers's *Mary Poppins* series and an older copy of the Dickens classic *Oliver Twist*.

As I left Charing Cross Road, I proceeded towards the only fully planned stop I had on my agenda. I had decided that, instead of taking in a hodgepodge of typical tourist sights, I would spend my time attempting to gain more intimate knowledge on a single specific topic.

This was not the first time I had approached travel in this manner. On a previous trip to England, Laura and I had spent a day visiting the old haunts of Jack the Ripper. (As you might guess, this was my idea, not my wife's.) I call this type of travel "theme tourism."

This time around, I had decided to indulge myself in seeing whatever was left of the world of Charles Dickens.

I think both Thom and I first became interested in Charles Dickens because of the *Mister Magoo Christmas Carol*. We would watch this cartoon version of the Dickens classic each year as part of our holiday tradition. And although it was eventually replaced by the Burl Ives version of *Rudolf, the Red-Nosed Reindeer* as the most anticipated television event of the season, it nonetheless left an impression.

The Dickens connection was later strengthened by my forced fifth-grade reading of *Great Expectations*, a book I thoroughly enjoyed primarily because of an odd physical attraction I felt toward the literary description of Estelle, the story's heroine. And it was sealed several years later by my sister's obsession with the *Oliver!* movie soundtrack. I can still sing most of the score to that film and will, even today, occasionally break my sister up with a well rehearsed imitation of the title character's famous request, "Please, sir, I want some more."

I soon graduated from cartoons and movie musicals to chunky paperbacks and, eventually, more durable hardcover versions of Dickens's novels. Over the years I have managed to read (and reread) the entirety of his collected works, as well as several biographies. My ongoing interest in the author caused me to seek him out in this place where he lived so many years, and there could not have been a better place to start my pilgrimage than the Dickens House Museum on Doughty Street.

The museum is located in the three-story townhouse where Charles Dickens resided from 1837 to 1839. During his stay at this upscale address, he worked on at least seven major books, including *Oliver Twist, The Pickwick Papers,* and *Nicholas Nickleby.* The building today houses a wide variety of memorabilia and, if you have a credentialed scholarly interest, a collection of letters and manuscripts by Dickens that may be accessed from the curator for research purposes. The most delightful feature of the museum, however, is its intimate atmosphere.

The museum staff are experts on the author's literary achievements, and—more important to me—they can converse about Dickens's life and his times in a way that brings him alive. I spent

CHARLES DICKENS

well over an hour talking to various staff members about one thing or another in relation to Dickens in London. And strangely, some of the stories of the author's youth had a very familiar ring.

———————◇———————

Although Dickens first lived in London in 1814 at the age of two, his life there did not really begin until many years later. In 1823, his father relocated the family back to the city after being transferred from his job as a payroll clerk for the British Navy. Young Charles was eleven at the time and because of money problems could not be sent back to school. His father, in fact, was sent first to King's Bench and then on to Marshalsea Debtor's Prison because he could not pay his bill to a wine merchant.

Mr. Dickens's incarceration was a misfortune for young Charles and, I would suppose, the tax-paying English public, but his father soon began to enjoy his situation. His creditors could not bother him, and he eventually arranged to have the whole family move in and share his cell. Even worse for the justice system attempting to mete out punishment, Charles's father was a civil-service employee at the time he was incarcerated and so could not be easily fired. Indeed, while enjoying the free room and board the jail afforded him and his family, Charles's father continued to collect his government paycheck inside the institution. The money he was paid allowed him to keep a maid in a small apartment a little way away from the prison so she could come to clean and care for the family's lodging.

Charles, himself, however, did not live in prison with his father; he remained at liberty and attempted to work and to return to school. He found work at Warren's blacking factory, where he helped to make shoe coloring for the paltry sum of six shillings a week.

Now, I cannot say that I know what it's like to work in a blacking factory—a circumstance that was apparently humiliating to the young Dickens. But in the realm of jobs for preteen boys, the blacking factory is very likely analogous to a small town paper route, a job of which my brother and I can speak with some authority. Thom, in fact, worked two routes at one time, bringing home about thirty dollars a month—surely the 1970s equivalent of six shillings a week.

Thom met his wife Nanette while working his deliveries, so I suppose the route compensated him in ways that went beyond simple monetary gain. Then again, my sister burned out the clutch of the family's compact car on the Placerville hills while helping Thom deliver papers on rainy days. I suppose on God's divine balance scales, the paper route exacted its payment for the romantic opportunities it provided.

The Dickens family was finally released from debtor's prison when Charles's grandmother died and the British government seized the inheritance to pay Mr. Dickens's debt. Charles, by that time, had managed to go back in school, where he stayed until 1827, when the family's cash disappeared again. This time Charles, who was fifteen, took a job as a solicitor's clerk. He was apparently not cut out for an office position; he spent many afternoons throwing cherry stones out of the window, trying to drop them into the hats of ladies who were passing by.

Neither was this sort of workplace high jinks unfamiliar to Thom or myself during the various periods of our employment. The most notorious of these tales would have to be the day my father, who at that time (army skills aside) was helping manage his friend's pizza parlor, hired Thom and me as teenagers to man the restaurant for an afternoon. It turned out that the greatest concern of the shift was not so much whether customers were satisfied, but what might happen if a full box of wooden matchheads were compressed in a ball of tin foil and then thrown into a brick-lined pizza oven. The bricks survived largely intact, and, thankfully, the local fire marshall was not a customer that day.

Charles Dickens, for his part, eventually left his position in the law firm and took a job as a Parliamentary reporter.

In 1829, prior to his first literary success, Charles found himself at a major turning point in his life. It was then, at the age of seventeen, that he had his first great love affair. The woman who had captivated young Charles flirted unmercifully with him, yet would not commit to a stable relationship. So, as any good romantic artist would, Charles began to go to extremes to win her affections. As Van Gogh cut off an ear and Toulouse–Lautrec drank himself to death, Dickens decided to become an actor—and all for the love of a woman.

And then, there was my brother . . .

––––––––––––––––––⬦––––––––––––––––––

Before Nanette and Thom were married, they were childhood sweethearts. Since their very first meeting, she had an unsettling effect on him and his sensibilities.

I still remember the aftermath of Thom's first vision of his then future wife. He was out soliciting newspaper subscriptions in her neighborhood, attempting to increase the size of his route. He knocked at the door of a house that had been owned for years by a family Thom and I knew well. He expected that, barring an adult, a rather gangly teenage boy or his tomboy sister would be answering the door. The house, however, had been sold, and the new owners, the Willey family, had already moved in. Nanette Willey, who was leaving for a swim party and was expecting a girlfriend to be knocking, answered the door in her brand new bikini. Though only twelve years of age, she was an eye–catcher in a swimsuit, and my brother spent the next several days in a sort of trance, constantly shaking his head and muttering to himself.

Within a month, I witnessed Thom and Nanette being "married" by an eighth grader named Igor O'Reilly at a Sadie Hawkins dance. The ceremony involved paying the "justice of the peace" a dollar and exchanging a kiss in front of a cheering crowd of observers. Thom had won Nanette's heart.

As time passed, Thom and Nanette went their separate ways. Thom moved on to Berkeley and then to Los Angeles to study art, eventually finding work painting for the motion–picture industry. Nanette went off to college to prepare for a career in nursing. Even in this interim, however, whenever I talked to Thom, he invariably filled me in on "the Nanette situation." The information would be secondhand, retrieved from old mutual acquaintances in Placerville,

Tower Bridge

but he always shared it excitedly, and the conversation always seemed of great importance.

More time passed. It was 1981, and "the Nanette situation," as I understood it, looked bad. She would be graduating soon, and my brother, so far removed, seemed all but forgotten.

Then it happened. As my brother tells it, he awoke with a start one night having had a dream that he had called Nanette. So the next morning he did just that. Thom phoned her parents' house, the only number he knew, and hoped that they not only still lived there but would answer and give him Nanette's current listing. To his delight, he did not have ask for her new number, nor did he have to make a second call; Nanette answered the phone. She was home recuperating from a broken leg and emotional drain from the demands of college.

Nanette was happy to hear from Thom, and they made a date to meet the very next weekend. The only obstacles facing my brother now in securing a divinely inspired reunion with his true love were simple logistical ones—such as the fact that Thom lived five hundred miles away from where Nanette was staying, that a motorcycle was his only transportation, and that he was tied to a film production schedule that would only allow him forty-eight hours away! But Thom has never been the type to be daunted by such trivialities.

Most guys I know have stories of times they went all out and emptied the bank account just to impress some girl on a date. I myself once spent several hundred dollars to buy Neil Diamond tickets from a scalper just because the woman I was seeing had expressed an interest. (I found later that this woman, who became my wife, had only a marginal interest in the performance and that I could have won her just as easily at the dollar matinee.) My efforts pale, however, in comparison to my brother's efforts on this particular adventure.

To begin with, Thom decided that his motorcycle was unsuitable for the occasion. He had to have a car he would look good in—naturally, that ruled out an AMC Pacer. He also needed a cassette deck so that he could play Nanette's and his favorite song from junior high, "Moon Shadow." A white sports coupe was selected. Thom drained his savings and paid cash for the car. The date had begun to take on legendary proportions.

Next, wanting to get Nanette away from the physical and emotional burdens she was carrying, Thom decided to take her to Lake Tahoe, conveniently located in the mountains above Placerville. The choice would add two to three hundred miles onto the one thousand he would be driving over the two days he had for the visit. But he figured the time on the road would be just right for getting reacquainted. He made reservations for dinner and dancing and left Los Angeles early on Saturday morning. He arrived in Placerville just in time to freshen up, collect Nanette, and whisk her off toward the lake in hopes of making his dinner reservation.

Nanette, Thom says, looked beautiful even in her leg cast, and they danced until the early morning hours—all the while contending with the crutches she was forced to use for support and balance. The talk on the drive back down from the mountains lasted even longer in Nanette's driveway and ran on into the next day. When Thom left the following afternoon, he and Nanette had both come to fully appreciate what each had always known: They were destined for each other.

As much as it pained him to leave her, Thom had to get back to Los Angeles. Movie production schedules do not wait, even for youthful romance. Thom had not slept in more than thirty hours and was ten hours away from where he needed to be. Still, as he describes it, the turn of events had so enraptured him that he barely noticed the miles. He arrived in southern California with just enough time to drive to the production studio and sleep an hour or so in the parking lot before his work day began.

This commute, needless to say, became a regular weekend event. And even though the first date had cost roughly seven thousand dollars, according to my brother's tally, the net result was that he had won the heart of his future wife.

Charles Dickens did not make his fame on the stage, although he remained active in amateur productions through most of his life. And he did not marry that young woman who captured his heart, but settled into a union with a woman named Catherine Hogarth that would produce ten children but end in separation. What he did do was write wonderful stories, beginning with the first *Sketches from Boz* in 1833 and ending with *The Mystery of Edwin Drood*, left unfinished at his death in 1870. The years in between saw the production of at least fifteen major novels, plus a variety of stories, articles, and lectures. And most of those wonderful works were created right in the heart of London.

Dickens lived in the city for thirty-seven years before finally separating from his wife and moving to Gadhill Place near Rochester

in Kent. Although he lived in several houses during those years, most have been demolished, as have been the schools he attended and the places of business where he worked. A pub or two that he used to frequent can be located—one is the White Swan Inn—and The Old Curiosity Shop still exists as a recreation of the one Dickens knew.

The best sense of Charles Dickens's London can probably be gained on the streets he used to walk so vigorously. Putting in miles a day to sort through problems and work through creative efforts, the author learned the city by moving through its arteries, not by watching it pass him by from a window. On these same streets today, in a deep London fog, one can easily imagine that the Artful Dodger is still lurking about, sneaking his haul back to his master Fagin, or that Ebenezer Scrooge is scurrying down the lane to buy the Cratchits a Christmas turkey. The brick buildings still hover close to the street, concealing secrets in their shadows. The vendors call from open-air markets and streetside stalls with the same cheery shrillness as those who called to the novelist on his walks around London, and the tantalizing smell of charring "bangers" (sausages) and onions still tickles the nostrils of anyone who passes by.

Charles Dickens has long been at rest in the Poet's Corner of Westminster Abbey. But his world seems to live on forever in the streets of London and in the imaginations of those who read his stories.

———————◇———————

During my wanderings about Dickens's London, I happened across an interesting pub called The Fortune of War, located across the street from St. Bartholomew's Hospital and down the street from the priory church dedicated to the same saint.

During the eighteen hundreds, the establishment was a market-place for what Dickens called "resurrectionists." Also called body snatchers, these entrepreneurs would raid local cemeteries for cadavers to sell to the hospital's medical students. Several stone benches still line the pub's upstairs rooms; on these the corpses would be posed, waiting for inspection.

As if that weren't enough, the street corner where the pub is situated, called "pie corner," is where the Great Fire of London burned itself back into control. The blaze, which started on Pudding Lane near London Bridge, also burned as far as Poultry Street over its four-day life in 1666. This disaster destroyed some fifteen thousand structures and left a hundred thousand people homeless.

With pudding, pie, and poultry all being baked or charred from the heat, I wondered if it might also have lead to the tradition of the outdoor barbecue.

As I sat at the Fortune of War pub, gazing at my half-empty flagon of warm English ale, I mused about the many absurd and sublime components of this great city. What explains the magnetic appeal of London? What mysteries and rewards draws the multitudes to its winding streets and hidden lanes? My companion, the glass of ale, could supply no answers.

When a man is tired
of London, he is tired of life;
for there is in London all
that life can afford.

SAMUEL JOHNSON
quoted in *Boswell's Life of Johnson*

VIII

Tales from the Road

MANY HAVE OBSERVED that in a world filled with televisions, both our written and our oral traditions are in danger of dying. Yet, those who would imagine that storytellers and yarn spinners are completely a thing of the past would find that their demise has been greatly exaggerated. Almost everyone I have met on the road knows a story or two and, with the proper encouragement, is more than willing to share the tales.

This prompting may take the form of flattery. Or it may be that a bit of "bending an elbow" might be necessary to loosen a tongue. But most often, I have found, it is simply a willingness to listen that turns the most withdrawn individual into a modern-day bard.

Although there are many types of story that can be collected, I have a tendency to ask my tellers for ghost stories and legends. I do not know where this particular interest comes from, so I cannot really rationalize the fascination. But, the Tower of London was to my mind an obvious place where one might hear a ghost story or two. Some time ago—I do not remember when or where—I had been told that the Tower was haunted by Anne Boleyn, the beheaded wife of Henry the VIII. I thought that those in charge of the old fortress might be able to tell me something of the ex-queen's alleged antics since her death.

As it turns out, if Anne Boleyn does haunt the Tower, she is far from lonely. The Tower of London is considered by some to be the most haunted place in all of England, a sort of Ramada Inn for the dearly departed.

I sat in front of the Tower for some time before I found a "yeoman warder" who seemed idle enough to be willing to talk. He was

dressed as British tradition would dictate and truly lived up to the image of the "beefeater," the popular nickname for these particular guardsmen. Whether from cattle consumption, as the nickname would suggest, or just from an extreme taste for Häagen–Dazs, the gentleman had lost much of his military physique while standing post at the Tower. He nonetheless was patient with me and my questions and told an interesting story of a fellow yeoman who had a run–in with a pair of famous ghosts.

It happened well after the last tourist had left and the Tower had taken on its typical evening quiet. Those who remain within the walls at night are locked in, and the rest of the world is locked out. A young yeoman doing rounds near the Wakefield Tower heard a sound near the bird roost but could see nothing that might have caused the commotion.

The bird roost in the Tower of London houses several ravens that are permanent residents of the compound.
Legend has it that if these Tower ravens are ever lost, the Tower itself will fall and with it the kingdom. The young guard assumed that the ravenmaster, the birds' caretaker, was probably there doing his job, but he was taking his watch and the legend seriously and so walked through the darkness to investigate the disturbance. Approaching the ravens, he noticed that the sound became more distinct. It was not the rustle of the roost nor the caw of an individual bird, but the soft sound of somebody weeping.

Surprised at what he was hearing, the yeoman could only think that a young visitor had wandered off from a tour and become lost. It was a highly unlikely scenario, but the idea that a fellow guardsman was in there weeping sentimentally with the ravens was even less likely. Coming at last to a point where he felt he should have been able to see the source of the sound, the young yeoman saw only the dark roost and the staring black eyes of the birds.

The Raven   Tower of London

He might have shrugged the whole thing off, blaming the wind, his own jitters, or the nightly groans of the old building. But then the weeping began again, coming this time from the general direction of Traitor's Gate, the water portal through which many a condemned British citizen of old passed before meeting the axeman's blade on the Tower green.

Again the guard approached a point where he might have expected to see the source of the weeping, and again he found nothing. The sorrowful sound reoccurred twice more over the next several minutes, once at the so-called Bloody Tower and again, for a final time, at the White Tower, well within the central compound. Each time the investigating guard found nothing except the empty corners of the shadowed stone structures.

Giving up his chase, the guardsman went to report the incident to his superior and to enlist his help in the search. The officer, after listening to a recount of the evening's events, waved the young guard back to his post, telling him, "It's nothing but the princes."

Back at Wakefield Tower, where he had started his evening, the young yeomen again heard the crying. But now the guard called out in a comforting voice as he had been instructed, "Sleep now, boys. I'll keep you safe to the morning."

And then the sound trailed off into a peaceful quiet.

"The princes" to which the commander referred were the two young sons of Edward IV. After the king's death in 1483, twelve-year-old Edward was to be crowned King Edward V at the Tower. While preparations were being made, he and his younger brother stayed in the Bloody Tower at the request of their uncle, Richard, the Duke of Gloucester. When the time arrived for the coronation, however, Richard took the throne himself, usurping his nephew's position. The boys remained in the Bloody Tower for a time following the ceremony until they disappeared, apparently murdered by their uncle.

The details of the princes' deaths is still a matter of some controversy. In 1674, however, the bones of two children were found buried next to the White Tower and reinterred in Westminster Abbey as the remains of King Edward's two sons. Whatever the specific circumstances, it is apparent that the children died alone, afraid, and at the hand of someone they had known and trusted. According to my storyteller, their spirits still wander the Tower grounds hoping to find the comfort and safety they lacked while alive.

Though as a Christian I find the spiritual implications of such stories dubious, as a writer I can't help but marvel at the deliciousness of such mysteries.

———————◇———————

Leaving the Tower guards to their own ghosts, I next set out to find some haunting tales about old London manors and townhomes. Since private residences rarely employ guards, I knew I needed to find another source. Specifically, I needed a group of locals who might have an intimate knowledge of the city's residential areas and might be privy to the gossip shared down a neighborhood street or over a back fence.

At first, I was at a loss for ideas; I simply could not think of any such group. There are times when the light bulb in my head seems attached to a dimmer switch, so slow is it in illuminating anything.

When the idea finally struck me, however, it seemed so obvious.

What I needed was a mail carrier.

Postal carriers have usurped town switchboard operators as the primary conduits of secondhand information. My brother-in-law T.J., who has worked for the United States Postal Service seemingly forever, is a case in point.

T.J. is notorious for his knowledge about the comings and goings of everyone on his mail delivery route. In fact, he seems to know the major news of everyone who is served by his particular Los Angeles substation.

T. J. shares all his juiciest gossip with his fellow carriers during the morning mail sort, and his cohorts provide him with the same news service. T.J. even goes so far as to keep a short-wave radio scanner with him so that he can listen in on any emergency response chatter that might be broadcast in his neighborhood!

Having made this connection, I hurried to a place I had discovered a few hours earlier during my Dickens walk. Locals have dubbed this London common Postman's Park because it is the lunch spot of choice for many of the area's postal carriers. Indeed, one can easily become overwhelmed by the sight of so many postal employees gathered in one place. They don't exactly outnumber the pigeons in Trafalgar Square, but they do provide a rare insight into the herd behavior of civil service employees.

The fellows I approached were more than willing to spend a few minutes recounting some of their adventures. The only difficulty I encountered was in trying to focus the conversation.

It may be an effect of wearing a uniform, but I am convinced that in every mail carrier's body beats the heart of a closet police officer.

The talk in that park was at first so energized toward personal examples of postal heroism that I found it difficult even to bring up the subject of ghost stories. To give credit where credit is due, however, I will fully admit that I never knew mail carriers delivered so many babies, made so many arrests, or put out so many fires.

After several minutes of chat, the postal carriers finally began to consider my interest in any haunts they might have encountered or heard about during work days. Two stories emerged. The first involved a phantom dog that appears regularly at the statue of Peter Pan in Kensington Garden. The canine wraith will be heard barking furiously at the statue and then disappear into the distance, running toward Knightsbridge Road on the south side of the park. The story goes that the faithful animal is trying to lead any listener to his master, who fell victim to street crime in the fog of a London night.

The other story involved a professor's wife who lived off Russel Square in an old townhome close to the University of London. The woman had always been something of an eccentric, but with the death of her husband she also became a recluse. She would rarely leave the confines of her house except to shop for the few things she needed for herself and to look about the neighborhood for stray cats. She would take in the animals and care for the "lost lambs" as if they were her children.

So diligent was this woman in her efforts that, over the years, she eventually claimed ownership of hundreds of animals. One night, however, a terrible accident claimed her life. As she was walking down her back stairs to slip out into the evening and look for more strays, she stepped on one of her wards, fell down the incline, and broke her neck.

To this day, in the neighborhoods surrounding the house where this woman lived, cats who are left out at night will disappear. And at her old address, just as the sun fully sets, a cry and a crashing sound can be heard from the back of the house. After the replay of her fall is heard, the wail of mourning cats will fill the moonless London night.

———————————◇———————————

It was moving toward mid-afternoon, and I was beginning to yearn for both lunch and a seat. It seemed a good time to dodge into a pub for a quick snack.

I chose The Cockpit. Although it might be easy to assume otherwise from its name, the establishment was not run by an ex-pilot, nor was it decorated with antique aviator gear. It was rather named for the cockfights that used to be staged in that very place. The fighting ring for the birds (the "pit") was on the floor of the pub. Even though cockfighting was outlawed in England in 1849, the name has persisted.

The tavern was also of note for its unusual practice of enlisting ale conners to test its home brews. Conners are, in essence, highly skilled testers of an ale's quality. Through years of practice, they can discern the alcohol content in an ale through simple taste. So cultivated is a conner's palate that an establishment whose brew is being tested will be allowed to serve or be forced to destroy a quantity of beer on the conner's word alone.

Although to some hedonistic souls this might seem to be the perfect job, apparently there are days when even professional beer drinking can be trying. When an ale conner gets a cold, for instance, the ailment hampers the sense of taste so much that it cannot be depended on for the evaluation. In such a case, alternative means of testing have to be employed.

The most common substitute for taste testing involves pouring a quantity of the beer on a bench and then sitting in the puddle for several minutes. If the conner's trousers stick to the bench as the beer dries, the sugar content of the brew and, therefore, the fermentation and alcohol content has proven itself suitable, and the keg is judged ready for sale. If the pants do not stick, the beer is destroyed.

I myself have not had to sit in beer since my last undergraduate fraternity party—and then only as an amateur.

———————————◇———————————

Stories heard in the confines of a pub always need to be taken with a grain of salt, and this one is no different. Joseph, the story-teller, looked to me like a regular at The Cockpit. He knew the bar-keep, he knew the area, and he knew how to negotiate a free draft. He told me he was forty years old, but if this was true, they had been forty hard years. As I ate my lunch, Joseph tipped his glass bottom up. Then he settled back in his seat and smiled.

"So, you like to hear ghost stories?" He apparently was recount-ing as much of our conversation as he could remember.

"Not precisely," I responded. "I was wondering if you know of or have heard rumor of any local hauntings. I am hoping to hear about something that you or others believe to have actually hap-pened, not simply a story."

"The best stories are true," he agreed.

Smiling at this solemn attempt at philosophy, I again prompted him to share anything he might have heard.

"There's the robber's shadow . . ." he began.

I nodded my interest. So he went on.

A trio of street criminals living in the nineteenth century began acquiring such a large amount of ill-gotten booty that they could not possibly squander it all through their illicit enterprises. They needed a safe place to stash their excess cash, and they hit upon the brilliant idea of hiding it in the crumbling walls of the Priory Church of St. Bartholomew the Great.

This church had been standing since the sixteenth century and had survived everything from Henry the VIII's order for the disso-lution of the monasteries to the Great Fire of 1666. St. Bartholomew's was seen to be blessed even if it had fallen into disrepair. The rob-bers, therefore, thought it unlikely that anyone else would violate the sanctity of the church and happen upon their activities. Perhaps more important, the ruinous state of the building would allow them easy access to their hidden treasure on any given dark London night.

Unfortunately, as seems to be in the case in all robber relation-ships, a betrayal took place. One of the thieves took the lives of the other two in hopes of keeping the stash of valuables all for himself. But before this murderous thief could reclaim the loot, he too lost his life—a victim, ironically, of a mugging.

Since his death, many have reported seeing the robber's shadow on the wall of the old priory church. The shadow appears in the back lighting of a bright moon and points to the place on the wall where the thieves' treasure was sealed. The robber, having died before he could repent of the murders of his two friends, is trying to make amends for his sins by giving the money to the church in his death. Or so the story goes.

I walked out of The Cockpit, took a breath and mumbled some-thing to the effect of, "OK, I'll bite." I had just been told a whopper. It was a good one and told by a true fisherman. Since I was only a few blocks from St. Bartholomew's I decided to see if anyone there had heard of the "robber's shadow." I had a feeling I knew the answer, but it would cost me little time to find out.

The restored St. Bartholomew's is worth a visit. It is not as well known as many of the other churches of London, but it has a very interesting history and is still of some importance to the pomp and ceremony that surrounds the British royalty.

For one thing, St. Bartholomew's houses the altar of the Imperial Society of Knights Bachelor, who hold an annual service in the church every July. It was also the site where the British painter William Hogarth was baptized and still contains the font where that blessed event occurred. Enthusiasts of American history might be interested in knowing that Benjamin Franklin once worked in part of the chapel as a printer's assistant before it was reclaimed as a sanctuary.

The church also offers its share of oddities. For instance, it is the burial place of a very wealthy eighteenth-century hair merchant and wigmaker named Jonathan Thornell. So exaggerated and elaborate were Thornell's creations that he would recommend that the women who purchased his wigs set mousetraps in them at night to take care of any unwelcome guests.

ST. BARTHOLOMEW

Another interesting oddity is the annual activity of the Butterworth Charity. This entity still carries out the mandate Joshua Butterworth made in 1887 from the church. The philanthropist's desire was to help feed London's widows and orphans on an annual basis, so he set aside a sum to be used to buy and distribute food each Good Friday. His original allotment dwindled in value to the point where the sum will only afford the purchase of five hot-cross buns, yet these are still delivered annually to the endowment's designated beneficiaries. Each year the ceremony takes place on a flat tombstone that has always served as a table for the bounty provided.

Despite all of its fascinating lore, no one I talked to at the church could tell me anything about a robber's shadow at St. Bartholomew's. This is not to say, however, that the church is lacking in legends.

St. Bartholomew's, I was told by one of its attendants, is known for its spectacular collection of reliefs and statuary adorning its walls. As with many of the markers on the church floor, these carvings are commemorations or actual capstones to the crypts of buried dignitaries. One such marble edifice was of particular note for many years because it is was believed to be haunted by the spirit of the man whose likeness it portrayed. At night, when the silence of the sanctuary was complete, the statue would begin to cry. Tears would roll down its stone face, seeming to betray the emotions of the soul who was left in the grave beneath its pedestal.

Many who visited the church in those days witnessed the tears and suggested reasons for the disturbing occurrence. Little is known of the person whose remains were buried at this particular site, and so the speculation was wide and largely unfounded.

Some were certain that the statue was weeping for a lost love, one who had been separated from him for all eternity. Others offered that the grave had been mislabeled and the poor person resting beneath the monument was doomed to remain anonymous and forgotten to all the living. Happier interpretations speculated that the tears were shed in joy that the deceased had been buried in such a blessed place and with such notoriety when he had no station in life that would merit these rewards.

A simpler explanation for the crying statue has also been offered. Although the monument cried for years, it stopped abruptly when a gas furnace was installed in the church, and the tears have not returned since. Some would therefore suggest that the tears were a matter of water condensing on a cold stone face in a drafty old church in a foggy city.

Though this explanation makes logical sense, the writer in me longs to find another ghost story. Speaking from personal experience I can attest that, in London, nothing brightens the countenance like the miracles of central heating.

Perhaps the ghost was simply cold, and fixing the heating did wonders for his demeanor.

While yet a boy I sought
for ghosts, and sped
Through many a listening chamber,
cave and ruin,

And starlight wood,
with fearful steps pursuing
hopes of high talk with the
departed dead.

PERCY BYSSHE SHELLEY
The Indian Serenade

I X

The Invasion Begins

WE LEFT LONDON IN A HURRY.

We had managed to squeeze every last minute from our stay in the city, but rare scheduling concerns demanded that we vamoose. We had to reach the southern English coast by early evening, or we would miss our ferry to France.

We gave our rental car keys to the desk manager to attend to, then we settled our account. Or attempted to settle. We had to convince Dad that his call stateside that night *could* have been twelve minutes long rather than the "seven or eight at the most, Son" he insisted on. Since Thom was picking up the tab anyway, it seemed a moot point. But Dad is always one to check a bill for accuracy.

At last he conceded with his customary sigh, "Oh well, I don't know. . . ."

"Look at the bright side, Dad," offered Thom, "at least you were able to get through to home and catch up on the news."

This comment gave Dad the opportunity to volunteer an update on "his girls." It seems both Chihuahuas were fairing well, though one had settled into a general malaise which could only be attributed to loneliness. The dog had not been eating well, and was seemingly "a mere shadow of herself." This was hard to imagine given the ample bulk of the animal prior to departure. As we tried to take Dad's mind off his homesick mood, we flagged a cab and proceeded with the intricate task of loading.

Our assortment of luggage had grown considerably since we started, with boxes and bags accumulating as we traveled. It now must have numbered about eleven pieces, the total weight being roughly equivalent to the cab itself. Nevertheless, the driver was friendly and helpful, and it is surprising how much you can fit in one of those little cars.

Finishing with the bags, we loaded Dad. Though the shocks seemed to pretty much bottom out, the taxi still seemed fairly agile as it bolted into city traffic. Our driver knew his job and responded well to my brother's offer of a sizable tip (the phrase "a couple quid" was used), and he delivered us to the station with time to spare.

Having twenty minutes to kill, we glanced around the station and spotted a familiar bill of fare—for us at this time, a glimpse of heaven on earth. Indeed, although it is true that the road offers opportunity for novel experience and the potential for excitement in discovery, it is also true, as that wise philosopher Dorothy once noted, "There's no place like home."

In this case, it wasn't exactly *our* home, but it was the "Home of the Whopper," and to us it served as a worthy substitute. Swallowing the last of our burgers with a satisfaction that can only be described as "ugly" and "American," we left the Burger King as the boarding calls for our train began.

The romance of the rails has not been lost to the any of the Kinkade clan. Ever since my mother arranged for the family to take a local express from Placerville to San Francisco "just for the experience," trains have held a fascination for both my brother and me. This interest was probably sharpened because of the time we spent as children clambering around the railroad monument on Main Street in Placerville.

The monument was really nothing more than a steam locomotive and a coal tender that had been stationed at the entrance to Placerville's business district with the intent of enticing travelers to stop. Children from all over town used that old train as a transport for trips of imagination, pulling and pushing levers and throwing switches in the eternal hope that the great engine might eventually move. It never did, but we never stopped thinking that it might.

These childhood flights of fancy became real for my brother during his time as a "hoister"—a word coined by Thom and fellow artist James Gurney that can perhaps best be defined as a transient artist and adventurer. Riding the rails across America, Thom saw the hobo culture first hand and can recount train-hopping survival rules and rail etiquette as if his life still depended on it. (Once it actually did.)

"Never jump a car from the back," he told me, "because if you miss you will be thrown onto the train coupling and not survive the miss. Jump a car from the front, and a miss will bounce you against the side of the car and out from the train. You will be banged up but will still have all your limbs. An open boxcar is an invitation from the engineer; take advantage of it. Always check for the whereabouts of the yardbulls (railroad police) before you jump; they are the only people who will really give you trouble on a hop. Even on an open car, keep a low profile; bulls will occasionally ride a train to monitor it outside of the yard."

My brother learned some of these rules by listening to those he met along the road, but he learned many others through the harsh lessons of personal experience. While riding a freight train through Ohio, for example, Thom decided to enjoy the vistas of the broad plains. He and Jim made their way to a flat car at the back of the train and sat there talking and enjoying the scenery. The brisk rush of air from the sixty miles-per-hour freight spawned the notion that flying a kite off the back of the train would be a nice addition to the relaxed atmosphere of the early evening. A kite was fashioned from sketch paper, and packing twine from Thom's sketch kit provided the tether.

While it is true that kite flying can be a peaceful and rejuvenating experience, it is just as true that any object lofted two hundred feet in the air will be noticed by even casual and disinterested observers. This is *especially* true of objects lofted two hundred feet off the back of a train where nothing and nobody should be present.

Needless to say, my brother and Jim were discovered as unwelcome stowaways. That they were evicted from the train at the next yard and not tossed bodily from the moving car is a mercy for which we are all thankful.

This is not to say that the yardbull will always get the best of a hobo encounter. Several days later, during this same trip, after Jim and Thom had been tossed from yet another train, they happened upon an advertisement on the rail yard bulletin board soliciting drivers to deliver a company-owned truck to New York City.

The two evicted hobos applied for the job, were accepted without much question, and drove out of the train yard in a truck owned by the very rail system from which they had just been tossed. In a gesture of good-natured payback, they startled the yardbull who had just removed them from the train by honking and waving from the new transportation his company had provided them. They heard his tirade of expletives all the way out the train yard.

In a side note, the company truck in question was an emergency vehicle equipped with siren, emergency lights, and auxiliary steel wheels front and back that would allow the vehicle to actually drive on the rails. Entrusting this truck to the two inveterate adventurers was a risky move on the part of the rail company. For more than a few miles, the road to New York was accomplished while screaming down the tracks at eighty miles an hour, auxiliary wheels down, siren roaring, lights flashing, and two young hobos laughing riotously inside. Only after a near head-on with an express freight did the truck return permanently to conventional streets.

The train was crowded. After dropping our luggage in the baggage car, Thom, Dad, and I walked from one end to the other in search of seats. We found only two, and these were spaced far apart among the hundreds of passengers. We left Dad at the first we found, Thom took the second, and I headed off back toward the baggage car.

I did not mind the lack of a seat. The baggage compartment on this commuter train offered welcome solitude and a place to stretch out for a few minutes. My long day of wandering in London was taking its toll, and I was beginning to wear around the edges.

I pushed around a few bags, grabbed my own as a pillow, lay out on the floor, and was letting the rhythm of the ride lull me into a delightful doze when I heard the voice.

"Hey, Pat. Let's hit the dining car and see if we can scare up any adventures." My brother's energies sometimes amaze me.

I was not sure I had the strength to go looking for adventure at that moment, but I responded nevertheless. As it happened, we really did not have to look far.

The dining car was nothing more than a bar disguised as cafeteria. Pretzels and warm three-day-old egg salad could be bought if anyone really had the desire, but the assembled crowd was really there to drink away the trip time and gain the strength to face whatever circumstance awaited at home. It was a tough room.

MAN ON
TRAIN
ENGLAND

In the center of this group of hardened urban commuters was a situation that seemed to be reaching critical mass. A loud and loutish fellow was waving a dark English brew and commenting on anything that was within shouting distance. My brother, for reasons that are his alone, gravitated toward this epicenter and sat down. The fellow in question acknowledged the approach and immediately raised his glass to Thom in salute.

There is a Chinese proverb which suggests, "He who drinks
with a fire-breathing dragon does not often wish to toast," but my
brother ordered a coffee and raised his glass in turn. A relationship
of sorts was formed. In the back of my mind the oft-quoted line
began resonating, "Hang on, boys. It's going to be a bumpy night."

Alan, as his friend George introduced him to me, was dressed as
a typical businessman but had the personality of an English soccer
hooligan on a rampage after his team had lost the World Cup. As if it
were appropriate to begin all casual conversation in such a way, Alan
began our conversation with a direct attack on my brother's mustache.

"Is that a mustache, or is that a rat asleep on your lip?" Alan
asked.

I am not sure why the mustache irritated Alan so much—it is,
after all, just a mustache. There were two beats of extremely uncomfortable silence after this rather odd opening. It seemed as if everyone was sizing everyone else up. If this had been a saloon in a
Western movie, the honky-tonk piano would have stopped, everyone would have gone silent, and the two principal antagonists would
have been slowly motioning toward their guns.

As for me, I was struck with a strong sense of deja vu. Thom
and I, on one of my visits to his house in Placerville, were at a tavern in a nearby country town when we were mistaken for two
undercover police officers. It is a long tale to tell, but the gist of it is
that, out of the blue, the tavern regulars accused us of being "narcs,"
confronted us with pool cues raised as weapons, and asked us in
impolite tones to leave. In that circumstance, we did so with a certain haste, though we couldn't resist a humorous revenge. Stopping
at a nearby pay phone, we called the establishment and announced to
the proprietor that those two men were indeed undercover opera-
tives and that a raid would soon be in progress. We laughed as we
drove back by the roadhouse and noticed that the parking lot was
empty and the lights were completely out though it was only 9:15 P.M.

On the train, routes of exit were less available than at the road-house, so in this case escape seemed unlikely and response seemed necessary. Thom, who is very secure in such situations, replied to Alan's rather odd insult by introducing himself and asking his assailant about his life. It seemed to be the right response. Alan laughed, clapped Thom on the back, and offered to buy a round. The piano started playing again; the card players and saloon girls picked up their conversations where they had left them moments before. The gunfight had been avoided.

For the rest of the ride we talked to Alan and George about everything and nothing. Topics included our trip, their jobs, the history of World War II, and, incongruously, international fishing rights. As the time passed and the train made its stops, the crowd thinned. Thom recorded Alan's craggy face in his sketchbook during our conversation, and I was again reminded of the fine art of conversation exuded by the British. At the second to the last stop, Alan bid us farewell. As he made his way down the ramp, Thom caught his attention.

"Before you go, I need to ask you something," Thom said from the window.

"What's that, lad?"

Thom's response was classic: "Are those eyebrows, or have two mice built nests on your forehead?"

The door shut before Alan could answer. A wise soldier times his shots well.

———————◇———————

Speaking of soldiers, our own D-Day was at hand. In another hour the train arrived at Portsmouth, and it was time to embark on a journey into our father's memories of World War II.

Portsmouth has a long seafaring tradition. Ships such as Henry the VIII's *Mary Rose* and Horatio Nelson's flagship the *H.M.S. Victory* have found permanent berths in the city's Naval Heritage

Center and can be toured by the public. We, however, were not drawn to Portsmouth for the experience of British naval history. We came because this was the staging area for my father's deployment to France in 1944 and the gateway for our own excursion into Europe.

We taxied from our train directly to the ferry that would take us across the English Channel to Cherbourg, France. As it turned out, the boat on which we would be traveling was a behemoth, offering many of the same amenities that one would expect on a pleasure cruise. It boasted several restaurants, including one that advertised itself as "fine dining."

Although I did not eat in this particular establishment, I did take opportunity to investigate its self-description. I think the most apt description for what I found might be stated as "buffet by candle-light." The dessert cart had a sign pointing to it designating it as "self-serve" and turned out to be nothing more than a chest freezer holding ice cream bars. The "gourmet" salad bar consisted of some wilted lettuce, a bowl of cherry tomatoes, and the largest mountain of watercrest I've yet seen in one place. In sum, although it could be called dining, I question the idea of fine.

Beyond culinary pastimes, the ship also offered varied entertainments. Several movie theaters were on board, a small casino was in operation, and a large cabaret opened for business as soon as we left port. Thom, Dad, and I decided to settle in the cabaret for the evening. After a floor show that showcased the rock-and-roll music of 1950s America as only the French can sing it, we had another chance to resurrect Dad's past visit to England and his passage to France all those years ago.

<hr />

After my father arrived from America in Boothe, England, he and the rest of his company were immediately transported to Bishop's Stortford, the site of an airfield just to the north of London. Here, with friends he had made in basic training, Dad was to spend six months before being dropped on the beach at Normandy.

Seymour Weiss, Al Bush, Charles Raffkey, Bernard Armbrester, and Dad had become a "pack," and as such they ran, yelled, fought, and tore up the town during their stay in Bishop's Stortford. My father winks and laughs that some of the stories from their three-day passes to London are interesting, some are hair-raising, and some are downright unprintable.

"The only one of us who got into real trouble was Raffkey," Dad pointed out. "He forgot to come back from a leave and stayed in London for an extra five days." The man ended up loosing a full rank because of this minor oversight.

My dad always managed to make it back to the base before his leave ran out. "Granted," he admits, "there were times I just barely made it, and then only through the grace of a hitched ride that replaced a missed train, but somehow I was always there for Monday morning review."

This is not to say that Dad stayed out of trouble during his stay in England. Indeed, it was during this period, not his time in the European campaign, that my father's life was in the most jeopardy. Over this relatively short period of time he was hospitalized twice and nearly a third time for "friendly mishaps."

The first visit to the hospital was due to a case of stomach cramps. From Dad's description, this was not an "Oh, I wish I hadn't eaten those clams from the beach vendor" sort of discomfort. This was industrial-strength, United-States-Army-issue gastric distress that put Dad in the hospital for two weeks recovering from its effects. He still wonders how, out of the three thousand men who were eating at that particular bivouac, he managed to be the only one taken ill, especially since we Kinkades are legendary for our strong stomachs. I wonder if it wasn't a practical joke played on him by his pack of friends that got out of hand. The "maxi-lax" in the food of a buddy is, after all, a classic prank.

The second hospitalization was even more serious than the first, and again served to demonstrate the sensitivity and the understanding of a buddy relationship. During his time in England, my father spent some time learning to repair airplane hydraulic systems. This translates into a lot of time spent in and around hangers. Dad was on duty just outside one of these hangers, standing right in front of its door, when an air-raid siren went off.

For reasons that remain unclear, when the warning signal sounded, another solder in Dad's company jumped into a jeep and tried to speed away. The jeep and its driver drove straight into a cable that attached the hanger door to the three-ton truck used to move this gating up and down. The jeep hit the cable with such force that it pulled the door free from its tracking and outward at a high velocity. As my father calmly observed this incident while taking a drag from a borrowed cigarette, the flying hanger door hit him sharply on the forehead and threw him thirty feet, crumpling him onto the runway.

When Dad awoke, Seymour Weiss was lifting him up and calling his name. He tried to open his eyes but could see nothing and feel little. In a daze that was rapidly turning to panic, he asked his friend, "Are my eyes gone?"

Weiss answered, "Ah, heck, Bill, your eyes are still there, but your head is all swelled up like a balloon!"

Dad took a final puff on his Camel, then passed out. He awoke next in a hospital with a medic talking over him, saying he was going to feel a slight prick and then a numbing sensation. Dad knew what this meant; he was going to get some premeasured morphine injections from an army medical kit. He received two, one in each side of his neck, and when he awoke again he was in a hospital with a few new scars in his face to help him remember the day.

Two weeks later, an army psychiatrist came to Dad's bed and asked him three questions.

"What's your name?" asked the army doctor.

"William Thomas Kinkade II," answered my father.

"Where were you born?"

"St. Louis."

"Who was the twelfth President of the United States?"

"Abraham Lincoln."

"Son, you're ready for regular duty."

From this thorough examination it was determined that, although my father's head had indeed enlarged to the size of a balloon, no real damage had been done. He was ready for action.

On 6 June 1944, the Allies landed on the shores of France at Utah, Omaha, Gold, Juno, and Sword Beaches; this was the beginning of the Normandy Invasion and the push that would eventually win the war in Europe. Thirty days later, on 6 July, my father received notification on the company bulletin board that he and his friends were to join the assault. His company packed and were transported to Portsmouth. At three o'clock in the afternoon they boarded a converted passenger ship for the voyage to France.

The passage was long, lasting about twenty-five hours, and uncomfortable. The sea was rough, and the ship was crowded. Soldiers were lying everywhere, trying to rest and to keep down their K-rations. When the call came to unload, it was about four o'clock the next day, and it was then that my father nearly hospitalized himself for the third time before he had faced a single enemy soldier.

Climbing down a cargo net off a ship to a landing craft was a practiced procedure for infantry and infantry support troops and had been done the same way by literally hundreds of thousands of soldiers since the invasion began. My dad, ever the trendsetter, decided to innovate. At the last minute, as he was climbing down the net, Dad decided that jumping the last few feet to the deck of the landing craft would add a certain bravado.

At the very moment of his decision, the boat he was jumping into was swallowed by a wave trough and fell about six feet from its original position. The six feet Dad had expected suddenly became twelve. He, along with his seventy–pound–pack, plummeted to the landing craft and, with all the grace that a Kinkade male can muster in such circumstance, landed on his rear end. He was certain he had broken his back, hip, tailbone, or all three. Luckily, Weiss was there to assess the damage.

"Ah, heck, Bill, your back's not broke. But your behind's all swelled up like a balloon!" Dad lit a Camel, took a drag, and passed out.

At this point, World War II was beginning to look to my father like a resort vacation compared to his experience in getting there.

Dad concluded his stories with the familiar sigh, "Well, Son, I don't know."

———————◇———————

We arrived in Cherbourg the next morning in much better shape than Dad had been in on his first trip across the Channel. We were rested, it was a sunny day, and our backsides had very little swelling.

We still, however, had the matter of contending with our grow–ing cache of luggage. We managed to find a luggage trolley roughly the size of a small pickup truck, and since no custom's official would have dared attempt an inspection of our mountain of suitcases, we simply walked through the port office. On arriving outdoors, we hailed a taxi and began the process of loading the eleven bags into the tiny French vehicle. This was a cause of great jesting and derision from the other cabbies in line who, like their English brothers, found it amazing that we Americans could possibly pack so much. Even more amazing is that all of us, to the last minute, still maintained we were packing light.

We instructed the taxi driver as to our destination, a local Avis rental office, and he sped away into the streets of Cherbourg. The town was still asleep as we wound our way through the lanes, but luckily the Avis office was open—something that had concerned us as we noticed how few businesses had begun their day. The man at the Avis office spoke little English, but we did manage to convey that our desire was to rent the biggest vehicle available. When he saw our pile of luggage he understood why.

He said something in broken English mixed with French and kept using the word *Nevada*. Thom began to explain that we were not from Nevada but still would like a large vehicle. At this he jumped unexpectedly up from the desk and pulled Thom bodily to the back of his garage, whereupon we finally discovered the meaning of his words. The vehicle he intended to rent us was a Nevada, manufactured, I believe, by Ford. The vehicle was indeed large by even American standards—a traditional full-size station wagon. Despite its size, the luggage still filled its interior to overflowing, and we were even tempted to strap a piece or two on top of the luggage rack. Dad, however, had plenty of room to stretch out his legs in the front seat.

Thom proceeded to communicate to the Avis attendant that we desired to return the car in Frankfurt, Germany. This, the man told us, could be arranged, though of course it would require special forms. These he could not find. We waited has he searched, made phone calls, searched again, found the forms, and proceeded to execute them. After writing for a minute or two, he stopped, made another phone call for instructions, and finally completed the paperwork. After handing Thom the keys, he shook his head in amusement and chuckled at the bedraggled American tourists.

As with virtually every vehicle we had entered in Europe, the combined bulk of our bodies and overflowing luggage overtaxed the suspension system to the point of near collapse. Our rear bumper scraped loudly as we drove onto the street. An old man walking up the sidewalk carrying a long loaf of bread noticed our departure. He, too, chuckled at the sight.

The Kinkades had landed in France.

————————◇————————

Having fully explored Cherbourg as a result of not having a map, we set about finding breakfast and orienting ourselves along the route my father had followed in his push toward Germany. Driving along the dockside, we had some difficulty finding a place to park. There seemed to be many vehicles in this location—probably local fishermen setting up shop for the day—but we could find no place to fit our sizable wagon. Finally we just left it parked on a small dirt area next to the sidewalk that ran along the waterfront. We then proceeded to walk about in the glorious sunshine. Seagulls were overhead, the small fishing boats were slowly rocking at their moorings, and the smell of fine French coffee was in the air.

We proceeded down the street to a small cafe whose sign announced that eggs and chips were available for twenty-nine francs. We headed indoors and sat with the sunshine streaming in while we consumed large plates of the advertised special. The eggs and chips were served with delicious French baguettes, accompanied with soft, sweet butter.

We had some difficulty at first communicating our desire to have our eggs over easy. But a gentleman was brought in from outdoors who spoke a bit more English than the waitress and who understood that we wanted our eggs fried. He nodded his head at the words "over easy" and proceeded to say, "Ah, yes, you want them well done."

We took several moments explaining that "over easy" was not a euphemism for the phrase "well done," but that it meant eggs with soft yolks. He gradually understood this, though when our eggs came we found that *his* translation seemed a more accurate description of what we were served. Nonetheless, when cut up along with the French-fried potatoes and mixed with a liberal dose of tomato ketchup (which they were quick to serve us, despite the fact we hadn't asked for it—after all, we're Americans), the resulting mixture was quite palatable and filled our stomachs admirably.

As we left the restaurant, it did not take long to run into our first unexpected setback on the continent. Our car was completely blocked in. By this time Dad was very anxious to revisit the beach where he had experienced one of the truly defining moments of his life, but until the drivers of the cars surrounding us came to claim their vehicles, we were stuck.

Thom, always quick to take advantage of a spare moment, pulled out his sketchbook and began to draw. I decided to wander into the town center for a few minutes of exploration. Dad just paced about the area with the excited impatience of a child on Christmas morning waiting to open his presents.

I found a small flea market a few blocks away from our car's entrapment and enjoyed a few minutes of poking about the stalls and engaging in bilingual barter that seemed to amuse both seller and buyer. I bought some bread and fruit for the road and two small antique brass cats for my wife Laura and started back toward the car. When I arrived, Thom was just finishing his work, and Dad was about to explode.

CHERBOURG

Ste. Mère-Église

"Anybody show up?" I asked, knowing the answer.

"Nope," answered Thom, studying his now-completed effort. "But we're leaving anyway."

"How's that?"

"We're going down the sidewalk."

My first thought—that Thom was kidding—faded fast. The walkway in front of us was blocked along the side with pylons designed to keep traffic from driving up onto it from the street. With what Thom was proposing, they would work to keep us trapped on the walkway for a long, narrow stretch through a pedestrian area before we could exit to the street.

An American behind the wheel of a car is a nightmarish image for all Europeans. Thom, Dad, and I were about to reinforce the perception.

We climbed in the car, and with a casualness that did not betray what we saw as the absurdity of the moment, we began rolling down the sidewalk. The resultant image, an overloaded full-size station wagon with three ballcap-wearing American men casually driving down a crowded walkway while pedestrians kept pace on all sides is worthy of any *avant garde* film. Smiling and waving off a few people who got in our way, we managed the maneuver with only a few disturbed stares. For one tense moment we endured a face-off with a fish monger's cart, but the merchant backed off—after all, how could anyone survive a duel with a Nevada?

Dragging our tail loudly, we returned to the street and left the Cherbourg waterfront to the accompaniment of more stares and chuckles. We were finally on our way to the site of the most important invasion in world history. Thom put the gas peddle down, and the rear wheels chirped a bit as we pulled into traffic. "Yee-haw!" Thom yelled in mock Texan.

The driving is like the
driving of Jehu the son of Nimshi;
for he driveth furiously.

2 KINGS 9:20
The Holy Bible, King James Version

X

Fifty-One Years After D-Day

WE WERE STANDING ON OMAHA BEACH looking out toward the quiet surf. Dad was pointing up and down the coast, reminiscing about his specific landing and explaining some of the general history of the invasion. It was hard to envision the things he was describing. The only threat Thom and I felt as we stood there was from a hot sun and no sunscreen.

"Was this the place, Dad?" Thom asked.

"Yes, Son. Somewhere right along here I waded ashore."

"Does it look like the way you remember it?"

"No. It was so long ago, and there was so much happening. It's only familiar because I know I was here."

"What did it look like when you came ashore? What were you feeling?"

My father began trying to recount the story of his landing and his first hours in France, but it was difficult for him to do so. When Thom first suggested that he would take my father here, Dad had cried. He still seemed to be coming to grips with the emotions of this chance at a second visit.

Dad was twenty-five years old when he ran through the surf from his landing craft to Omaha Beach. His pack was heavy, the channel water was cold, he was tired, scared, and in some pain because of his fall. The battle line had been pushed ten miles ahead of the beachhead, but snipers still regularly shot from the coastal hills during the twilight hours.

It was about five o'clock in the afternoon when my father was directed toward the staging area where he and his company would begin their move to the front. The little village of Sainte-Mère-Église was about eight miles to the west. Dad's company was to march the road to this French town during the first part of the night, rest, and then truck out southward toward Chartres early the next morning.

By the time the march actually began, the shadows were already deepening, and by the time it was into full swing, the darkness was complete. The road was visible only through the flickering of hand-held blackout lights, which offered little to aid the marcher's sight but also offered little to aid a potential sniper's sighting. It was a trade-off that nobody questioned.

Dad described the march as looking like a stream of fireflies moving in slow motion into the distance. In other circumstances, he might have thought it beautiful. Now, however, his mind was filled with thoughts of death.

They had walked their first two miles past row after row of "rough boxes" stacked four deep and three high. Each box, Dad knew, held the remains of a soldier who had lost his life in the struggle to open the beaches and the road over which he now walked. The sight chilled and haunted him. Each step he took seemed to carry him deeper into darkness.

To the north and away from the beach were signs warning soldiers not to leave the marked road. The area was heavily mined with "Bouncing Betties," as the foot soldiers called them. If stepped on, one of these explosive devices would jump up about three feet before detonating, inflicting devastating injury to the unfortunate soldier who had discovered its hiding place. The area directly ahead of the marching soldiers had supposedly been cleared of mines, but the soldiers still took every step half-expecting the audible click that would begin the deadly sequence leading to an explosion.

DEVASTATED
FARMHOUSE,
NORMANDY

On both sides of the road were the telltale signs of battle. The buildings Dad passed were roofless, the walls were blown in, the earth itself was burned and scarred. At one point during this march, my father came upon the remains of a bull that had apparently been corralled near the point of an artillery blast. The animal had been thrown high into a tree and now hung lifeless from the branches.

Whether because of the blackness of the night or because he was distracted by his thoughts and his surroundings or because he, acting the Good Samaritan, offered to help a fellow soldier who was struggling with his pack, Dad eventually became separated from his company. He walked on past Sainte-Mère-Église through the French countryside and was well on his way to Cherbourg, ten miles to the north and the west of his ordered destination. Finally realizing his mistake, Dad began walking back over the distance he had just covered, hoping to reach his company before he was discovered missing.

It was two o'clock in the morning when he finally reached the point of exhaustion and simply began looking for a place to lie down. He was already five hours late for his proposed bivouac. Now he just hoped that he could find his company in the morning light and that his commander would be in a good frame of mind when he tried to explain his mistake.

About this time, he happened upon a parked flatbed truck and thought that it, compared to the damp ground, looked like a welcoming place to bed down for the night. He tossed his pack into the truck bed, climbed in after it, curled himself up into a ball, and slept fitfully until morning.

His next recollection is of the smell of coffee and the sound of low-talking voices. Sitting up in the truck, he looked around to see various members of his own company milling about, preparing what breakfast was available before the day's transport to Chartres.

Out of the thousands of soldier encampments in the area, it seemed, Dad had inadvertently wandered into his own. My father's guardian angel was apparently working overtime on this particular evening. Had his usual luck held, Dad undoubtedly would have ended up sleeping in a German truck heading for the Russian front.

After about an hour at Omaha Beach, we were ready to leave. Dad stooped to collect a small vial of sand, commenting briefly that "this beach took something from me, and I want some of it in return." Shrugging off further questions, he walked back up the beach toward the car.

Before leaving, we stopped for a picture in front of the large stone monument. Dad, in true military form, assumed the position of attention and even raised his hand in a proper salute. On an impulse, we gathered some sticks and carved "Corporal William T. Kinkade has returned" in the sand. Dad stood next to this makeshift monument and again we got photos.

I did a little collecting of my own—some small rocks and shells to give to my sons Zach and Nicky when they are older and can begin to appreciate where I found them. I also paused on the sands of Omaha Beach to make note of a few of Dad's stories. Such memories are part of a family's heritage, and I like to think in some small way I am helping to pass them on to future generations.

<hr />

After a short drive on roads with such names as Sargeant Hamm and Colonel Effler—named for fallen American soldiers—we arrived at the Normandy American Cemetery and Memorial. The site overlooks Omaha beach directly but allows vistas of Utah Beach and Gold Beach as well.

The memorial itself, a large bronze statue inscribed with the words, "The Spirit of American Youth," serves dutifully to commemorate the sacrifice of the young American men who lost their lives in this region during those first few weeks of the War for Europe. It is my feeling, however, that the statue pales in emotional impact to the stark simplicity of the graves placed in this hauntingly serene and naturally beautiful hilltop reserve.

I have visited military cemeteries on several occasions and have viewed war memorials on many others. I have stood before the Vietnam Memorial in Washington, D.C., and toured the Little Bighorn Grave Sites in Montana. In these visits and others like them, however, I have never felt so much understanding for the tragedy of war and the nobility of the warrior as I did on this occasion. The reserve is home to ten thousand small white Christian crosses and Jewish stars, neatly

CROSSES, NORMANDY

Dad Returns to St Mere-Eglise

arranged in rows and spread out as far as the eye can see. A shroud of quiet that no noise seems capable of penetrating is settled permanently over them. The only sound is the distant roar of the surf and the rustle of the ocean winds in the groves of cedar trees that somehow manage to stand against the ravages of the coastal weather. Here is a place where eternity seems to have found tangible form on earth.

I watched my father wandering up and down those rows and understood that it was here he felt the stab of fear, the horror of carnage, the pain of sudden loss. He also felt the camaraderie of fighting for a shared cause and the joy of liberation felt by those denied freedom.

"Be quiet in the midst of those who have fallen," a sign along the road read. "Honor the ones who gave their lives so you might be free." The silence was indeed transcendant. But Dad didn't see the sign. I saw him waving excitedly at me from four or five rows over.

"Where in Hades is the john, son?" he shouted.

Old soldiers never die; they just look for the nearest latrine.

———————◇———————

Fifty-one years ago, the little town of Sainte-Mère-Église had been my father's first official stop on the Voie de la Libération, the liberty highway. Now it was our next point of discovery on our exploration of the French countryside.

This quaint French village, like most small European towns, concentrates its social and economic life in the central town square. When we arrived, this town center was filled with the bustle of a farmer's market and the lively talk of friends gathered to share the latest gossip. The smell of grilling sausages and freshly picked fruits and vegetables wafted through the air. The mild case of melancholy that had settled over our collective sentiments since the Normandy memorials quickly vanished in the warm and congenial atmosphere.

In addition to its charming ambiance, Sainte-Mère-Église is noteworthy as the setting for a famous parachute landing of hundreds of American GIs, who proceeded to liberate the town a day after the D-Day invasion. Sainte-Mère-Église became known as the first French town liberated from the Germans during WWII and, we learned, is extremely proud of this particular claim to fame.

The village offers two primary points of interest to American travelers who are following the trail of the Normandy Invasion. The first of these is the Musée C-47, a museum dedicated to the American 101st and 282nd Airborne Divisions. It was these paratroopers who took the most active part in the liberation of this particular town and its people. The parachute-shaped museum offers a vast array of military hardware including a Sherman tank, various half-track personnel carriers, and the C-47 airplane that actually dropped the paratroopers over the town.

The museum was closed when we arrived, but when the curator was located and told of Dad's involvement in the war, we were allowed in for a free private viewing. Once inside, my father was in his element.

Over the years, Dad has picked up an incredible amount of trivia about the war and its associated artifacts. Viewing this as an appropriate opportunity, he proceeded to share this information with a gusto I had not seen in him in some time. At the same time, he began to display one of the idiosyncratic oddities of his storytelling style. I caught Thom's eye as Dad began talking us though the transmission gearing ratios of a military munitions carrier and the glide patterns of the plywood troop transports that were tethered behind larger powered aircraft. Thom smiled. We both recognized that we were hearing a textbook example of TMD, a conversational style in which one offers Too Much Detail. If you have a friend who shares his knowledge of the gestation patterns of kangaroos when you ask him if he has ever been to the local zoo, you have no doubt encountered TMD. This noncurable mental state seems to be most common in men and, as far as I can tell, gets much worse as the male ages.

"The plywood on these craft," Dad offered, "had to be laminated with a special resin to prevent air friction. It was tested to 320 degrees Fahrenheit under acetylene burners, then exposed to 460 mile-per-hour winds using concave tunnels with high velocity fans."

"I see," replied Thom. What other response could be offered?

After spending time at the museum, we made our way back to the car, first stopping at a curio store which featured vintage battle gear and other forms of war surplus sold as what amounted to antiques. Canteens, spent shell cases, field goggles, canisters of tear gas, various small arms, and even such objects as rusted nuts and bolts were all displayed in glass cases at exorbitant prices. The proprietor, a fat, jolly Frenchman named Jean Bernard, proceeded to welcome us to his store in his fine English and announced that since Dad was a veteran he had a special gift for him. After some searching about in cluttered boxes, he dramatically unveiled a medal that featured an upturned helmet in the sands of Omaha Beach and pinned this artifact on Dad's lapel. He further presented to Dad a postcard that depicted the scene a day or two after the initial invasion at Omaha

Beach. These two gifts were graciously offered in the spirit of thanks and appreciation for the part Dad had played in the great liberation.

As a special rite of initiation into the inner circle of his patrons, Jean Bernard even offered us access to the ultimate memorabilia in his collection.

"I can get you live German handgrenades for twenty percent off retail."

Though access to explosives is tempting to any Kinkade, we decided in the interest of safety to decline the offer.

Leaving the shop, we walked across the village square to the town church, the second landmark of specific interest for us. This charming house of worship is not a spectacular edifice in comparison to some that we had seen on this trip. It was established in the eleventh century and expanded significantly over the next three hundred years, taking on much of its present form in the fifteenth century. But the most unusual and striking feature of this place of worship is a recent addition—a set of elaborate windows that commemorate the town's liberation in brilliant stained glass.

St Mere Eglise

The north window in the church's transept, for instance, features a likeness of the Archangel Michael, the patron saint of paratroopers, surrounded by various religious symbols interspersed with military insignias. And the window that graces the southern and central entryway depicts an even more startling vision of Virgin and Child surrounded by a graceful garland of descending paratroopers, all hovering over the burning village. This window is so surreal that it took us a few moments to recognize all its features. Once we did, we all stood transfixed for quite awhile.

We learned later that these windows had been commissioned after the original medieval glass was destroyed in the battle. A famous craftsman was brought in to commemorate the town's most revered event, and the results of his efforts have gathered a worldwide following among aficionados of stained-glass art, not to mention aficionados of paratrooping.

As further reverence for the invading liberators, a full-sized paratrooper in battle regalia hanging from an unfurled parachute adorns the church, in effigy, throughout the warm months of the year. In fact, many postcards feature this church complete with the soldier hanging from its side, and this monument has become something of a local landmark.

Our experience of the church sparked another in my dad's armada of idiosyncrasies. This quirk of his spoken word might be called TLS or Time-Limited Sensitivity.

While wandering the church grounds, my father began to recount the certainly heroic and possibly tragic story of John Steele, one of the paratroopers who jumped into Sainte-Mère-Église on 5 June to attempt its liberation. Steele's parachute, the inspirational source for the hanging effigy, became caught on the church steeple, and there he hung throughout the night's long and vicious battle. The story goes that he was eventually "unbound" by a German solder named Rudolf May. Available records are unclear as to whether he survived the ordeal.

Dad described the event with a fierce and stirring intensity; he led us with his words into the horrors of the night and the special plight of this stranded unfortunate. However, when he brought us to the point where he would highlight Steele's ultimate fate, the time limit on Dad's sensitivity simply ran out.

"Tell us what happened!" we pleaded, expecting a sensitive account of the divine miracle that delivered the poor lost soul.

"They shot the living guts out of the poor guy," Dad replied matter of factly. "You boys ready to go?"

It was late afternoon, and we had finished our meandering about the town. The farmer's market had closed, and the number of townsfolk had dwindled to a few. At that point Thom decided to set up his easel and began to paint, drawing the traditional crowd that makes all artists an instant tourist attraction. My dad, sitting quietly, seemed content but tired in ways that seemed more to reflect his advancing age than the simple exertions of the day. I sat and watched them both, thinking.

My father was a young man in his twenties when he was last in Sainte-Mère-Église. His life was in front of him, and he felt invincible. I suspect he never thought of himself at eighty or wondered what the world would be like when he reached that age.

When my brother was twenty, he was just leaving college at the University of California at Berkeley to begin his career in the tough and unforgiving art market of southern California. He was a kid who managed to "rig" a box to the back of his motorcycle to help in the transport of portfolios or pizzas, depending on which "career" he was pursuing at the time. He acted invincible and I suppose that he, too, gave little thought to what he would be like at eighty.

Time on a day-to-day basis moves so slowly that it may not be noticed. Days can roll into each other, and a month can come and go with little change to mark its passing.

Life, on the other hand, passes quickly. Every time I take an opportunity to look back, so much has occurred that it is hard to reconcile the changes with what I had thought to expect.

My brother is not a kid, but a tourist attraction.

My father no longer has his whole life in front of him, but struggles against the loss of his youth.

A child approached my brother. "My father's shop," he said in hesitant English. He pointed to an establishment at the right of my brother's composition designated a "stop bar." At least art had the quality of eternity. In a few brush strokes a place and a moment in time could be preserved.

It was late, and we were on the road again. Our destination this time was Chartres, also called *ville d'art,* the artistic city. It is known for exquisite stained glass, skilled artisans, and a cathedral that is unsurpassed in divine majesty even when compared to the more famous Notre Dame. To us, it has also become known as "Shots." This reference came from my father, who is convinced, as only an American could be, that millions of French have been mispronouncing its name for the fifteen hundred years of the town's history.

We had not eaten since early in the day when we stopped for a small picnic of summer sausage and cheese in the square of Sainte-Mère-Église. We were all hungry again, so stopping for dinner seemed a great idea.

As fate would have it, in a country known for its superb cuisine and for the artistry of its chefs, the only place we could find to eat was a Chinese restaurant. It seemed a little out of place it the middle of the French countryside. Listening to a Vietnamese waitress phonetically pronouncing Chinese menu items in broken English with a French accent was a little bit beyond the average "grab a bite at Denney's" road stop.

Somehow, however, our choices were understood, and I can personally attest that the whole exchange was less difficult than placing an order in English at some of the local hasheries I have visited along

American highways. (The workers in these places often seem to have little command of any language at all.) However, when the German couple came in and sat behind us and started to speak in broken Spanish to our Vietnamese waitress, I did think she was going to pass out.

Finally, though, after a meal of fried rice, sweet–and–sour chicken, moo–shoo pork, and green tea as only the French can cook it, we were back on the road.

At this point in our journey, we were traveling along a wide, sweeping plain, an area that seemed almost devoid of any form of civilization. Occasionally a farmhouse appeared to serve as a mile-stone, but other than that there was not even much vegetation—the landscape had an almost eerie quality to it. After awhile, we spotted a fine point of light on the dark horizon. It almost looked like a star rising—a star of immense proportion. As we drew nearer, we realized it was a building, though still so distant that its form was indistinct. Two towers and a broad roof gradually came into view, shining like a beacon on a lighthouse as seen from way off at sea.

We had passed a roadmarker that announced that Chartres was twenty–three kilometers ahead. Surely what we were seeing could not be the cathedral, we reasoned, since at this great distance how could it possibly be visible? But as we approached, we were struck silent. All conversation ceased as we watched this spiritual revelation, this dramatic incarnation of the power and majesty of God loom larger and larger in our vision.

From the back seat of the car, my father's voice rumbled through the moment.

"Well, Pattypoo, what do you think of the church at old Shots?"

I closed my eyes and smiled. As readily as my dad translates the French "Chartres" into the American "Shots," he reduces this breath-taking cathedral to a "church," and his thirty–five–year–old son Patrick Timothy to "Pattypoo." My father is what might be affection-ately called a real piece of work.

Chartres at Dusk

This break in the emotional atmosphere allowed an opportunity to ask Dad what he knew of the structure's history. When asking this type of question, of course, I knew I was opening the door to yet another of my father's conversational idiosyncrasies. I have mentioned TMD and TLS, but AAC is clearly the most pronounced of these. His desire to Answer at All Costs is at the roots of several legendary moments in Kinkade family history.

The most famous of these came when nine–year–old Thom, while we were on a road trip to Santa Cruz, California, innocently asked Dad what was meant by the phrase, "Swing Low, Sweet Chariot."

My father never missed a beat. He earnestly explained that a chariot was a Roman vehicle and that swinging low referred to a pendulous action. "Swing low, sweet chariot" then, clearly indicated

Chartres

that the song's writer wanted to portray a "Roman vehicle perform-ing a pendulous action."

"Dad," Thom replied, "isn't it something more spiritual than that?"

Fortunately, we had pulled into the "Trees of Mystery," a local tourist attraction in the Santa Cruz mountains, before my father had a chance to further elaborate. Thom and I ran off to look at the trees while Dad mopped his brow behind us, having been spared the need to explain.

This night, when asked about Chartres, my father described in detail the differences between the two towers of the cathedral, one Romanesque and the other Gothic in architecture. He also explained that the cathedral building itself sits atop a small hill that rises out of the shallow valley where much of the town is located. This explained our striking view on approaching Chartres. The cathedral, on its rise, appears slightly elevated in relation to the plain and quite alone, with the rest of Chartres sinking from view into the hollow. At night, because of the lights shining on the structure, the cathedral lit-erally stands out against the darkness as a beacon.

All in all, it was an extremely informed and lucid discussion. I am still unsure how anyone outside of an art historian or cathedral curator would know the things that Dad told my brother. And of course I'm not totally sure that what he told us was *entirely* true.

As I mentioned, for better or worse, Dad is a real piece of work.

If you were there
no explanation is necessary;
if you were not, no amount
of explanation will suffice.

OMAHA BEACH MEMORIAL

X I

"Shots"

THERE IS AN OLD WIVES' TALE that suggests the French do not like Americans.

Our arrival in Chartres proved that at least some old wives know what they are talking about.

It might be passed off as the result of the late hour, but it was clear that the clerk at our selected hotel was not happy with our presence in her lobby. My brother, as is typical for him when initiating a casual conversation, opened the dialogue with a mild attempt at humor.

The woman behind the desk, in a voice designed to freeze mercury snapped, "Sir, do you want anything? I don't have time for this!" Thom looked back at me and shook his head; he was too tired to deal with an attitude this massive. I could only shrug my own resignation. Thom asked for three rooms. With obvious and heartfelt indignation, she proceeded to process our room numbers. I sat and wondered how Jerry Lewis would have handled the same problem.

Our arrival in "Shots" serves well as a metaphor for my father's two-month stay fifty-one years before—in a word, *trouble*. Some of the problems Dad experienced were typical to all the American soldiers living there. For example, there was the issue of cleanliness. In every respect, the American presence in "Shots" might have been described as "gamy." In fact, Dad claims that he and his comrades in arms often could not take baths for weeks at a time. Looking at the canals running about the old city and knowing that my father was in the area during the summer months, I cannot imagine why hygiene was abandoned by the American GIs stationed there, but apparently it was. On further reflection, I wonder whether this fact alone might have persuaded future generations of hotel clerks that Americans are undesirable guests and rendered them a bit surly.

My father's personal odyssey of mishaps, however, did not stop with simple dirt and skin problems. It got worse in ways that only he could arrange. In the relatively brief period of his stay, Dad had run-ins with both the town's sacred and secular authorities. It was probably a good thing, in fact, that he was transferred on to Paris and Cambrai before he caused the townspeople to rise up in revolt and demand that Chartres be reoccupied by the Germans.

As might be expected considering the circumstance, there were many shortages in "Shots" during the summer of 1944. Although a soldier who was friendly with the mess sergeant could have all the K-rations he wanted, such an arrangement was not exactly a bounty. A K-ration was basically a box of crackers, a tin of pork and beans, two cigarettes, two candy bars, and two pieces of hardtack. Fresh food was a real rarity.

Dad had been living off the boxed cuisine of the United States Army for several weeks when he happened to meet an old Frenchman who was in possession of a chicken. This chance encounter occurred during the early morning hours and seemed a blessing of the highest order. If there are chickens, he reasoned, there would have to be eggs, and if there were eggs, a semblance of a real breakfast could be assembled for the first time in a long while. Dad wasted no time in procuring all the eggs the farmer had for the princely sum of two packs of cigarettes.

Gathering his hard-won eggs, Dad walked further down the road looking for a place to cook them. As luck would have it, he happened upon a group of three soldiers squatting around a small fire and heating some water in a helmet for a shave. One soldier, in fact, had apparently just completed this morning ritual and was patting his face dry with a towel. Approaching, my father asked the other men if they would mind if he threw his eggs into their hot water to boil.

The two waiting their turn to use the water refused my father's request, not wanting the eggs to slow down their shaves. The third said nothing and only continued to wipe himself up.

My father has not always been a religious man and even now, though he has grown closer to God, is likely to use colorful language when he has been disappointed. In 1944, after being denied eggs for so long and then paying such an exorbitant price for those he had obtained, he was not about to let the soldiers refuse him this small request. He was, after all, a corporal, and they, from what he could see, were but lowly privates. Dad's litany of curses and expletives apparently would have curdled milk.

At about this time the third soldier, who had been turned away from Dad with his face buried in a towel, looked up from what he was doing and entered the fray. He, in fact, ended it.

"Son," he calmly said, "I want to see you in church this Sunday."

Father Scott Fitzgerald, an Army captain, was staring into my dad's eyes as only a Catholic priest and a military officer could. His look said something to the effect that if my father said another word, he would not only be digging latrines for the next two months, but would have to confess directly to Father Fitzgerald how he felt about the officer who gave him the duty.

The color left both my dad's language and his face as his new corporal's stripes wilted under the captain's directive. Dad was in church that Sunday and every Sunday for his entire stay at "Shots." Father Fitzgerald greeted Dad at the door before every sermon.

Although he never cooked his eggs, Dad did find a kind of religion that morning—the hard way.

Even despite his best intentions, my father's luck in "Shots," especially in relation to ranking officers, was destined to remain terrible. In addition to attending church under Captain Fitzgerald's watchful eye, Dad was also assigned to work for the colonel who was overseeing operations in the town.

The first order issued by this officer gave Dad the responsibility for refurbishing a building near the center of town that was to serve as army headquarters. The structure was in relatively good shape except for its roof, which had been rattled off during a bombardment just before Chartres' recapture, so the repair seemed a relatively straightforward task. The materials for the reconstruction were plentiful; numerous abandoned houses and buildings were nearby and could provide salvageable roof tile. And labor to complete the job was also easy to come by since German prisoners were being held in town. All Dad had to do was to acquire a transfer of custody for three or four prisoners, choose from among the bombed-out houses, have the prisoners dismantle the roof of the selected structure, and then have them use those tiles to rebuild the headquarters roof.

After surveying several of the nearby buildings, my father settled on one that was uphill from the headquarters. He felt that the transport of the heavy tile would be easier on a downgrade, with gravity doing much of the work. He sat and supervised while the German POWs began pulling down the tile and loading it onto the cart they were going to use for the transport.

After a few hours, Dad was mentally celebrating the success of his first assignment. Everything seemed to be going extremely well—until the shouting began.

It started as a distant commotion that seemed of no concern to my father or his workers. But as the ruckus grew louder and closer, Dad began to make out some of the heated words. A French local, it seemed, was gathering up the town police to have an American arrested. My father looked about to see if anyone was running from the direction of the disturbance and the presumed scene of the incident. He saw no one and so settled back to watch his workers, who by now had torn off about two-thirds of the roof.

Again the shouting picked up, this time from much closer. In fact, the people who were causing the commotion were now in sight. As Dad looked down the street, a man at the center of the small gathered crowd pointed up the street in his general direction. Dad turned to look past where he sat to see if the culprit were standing up the road from his position. He saw no one. Baffled, Dad turned back to see what was happening down the street.

The man who had pointed, three French police officers, and several onlookers were now walking briskly up toward him. Dad's face lost all color for the second time in as many weeks when the small collective of French nationals stopped directly in front of him.

In a most agitated tone, the man who seemed to be at the heart of the gathered group began waving his arms, grabbing his head, and shouting something about "damages to his home" and "demanding arrest." The ranking police officer interceded in this tirade by informing Dad in broken English that he was placing him "under arrest for looting and attempting to steal the roof off the home of a French national." The confusion got all the worse when the German POWs, who by now had also figured out what was happening, began calling to my father to shoot the Frenchman who had lodged the complaint.

As it happened, Dad was not arrested. He claimed to be acting under orders from the American commander in the area. He also promised to have his POWs put the roof back on the house of the aggrieved Frenchman.

The police graciously allowed my father this option.

———◇———

We awoke early the next morning. Our hostess from the night before was still on duty, but her sneer was tempered with the presence of another desk clerk. The new arrival was, unfortunately, only a bit more pleasant than the first, but he did steer us to a breakfast café that would serve "American tastes."

I assumed that meant we could again get ketchup for our eggs. I was right.

———◇———

After retrieving our car, we drove toward the outskirts of the city, attempting to circle the cathedral and find a good angle for Thom to set up his easel. We found this vantage point on the northeast edge of the town on the Rue de la Tannerie. Thom began his work, Dad sat down nearby to watch, and I once again set out to explore the area. The cathedral itself was only a few blocks from where we had stopped, so I headed in its general direction.

Three major water channels run through this area, and many colorful boathouses dotted the waterway along which I was walking. When I came across a small pedestrian bridge, I took the opportunity and crossed over toward the center of the city.

From the time and point I entered the old town I was truly lost. I have since tried to use a map to retrace the route I walked, but unscrambling my path through all the winding byways surrounding the cathedral has proved impossible. I can only say that whatever street I was on, it might have been called "Rue de la Loon." I have never seen so many psychologists advertising their practice in such a compact area in all my life and travels—and I have wandered both in Sigmund Freud's Vienna and Woody Allen's Manhattan. The average citizen of Chartres is either extremely neurotic or extremely well in touch with his or her "inner child." In either case, they must be putting in a lot of couch time to support the professional community into which I wandered.

Entering between two massive and architecturally distinct towers, I passed through the "Royal Portal." The three sets of doors that make up this entrance feature full-length carved reliefs of the kings and queens of Judah, Jesus' royal ancestors and his spiritual forebearers.

Yet, as truly impressive as this was, it did not prepare me for my first sight of the cathedral's interior. Like the other visitors around me I could for a moment do nothing but simply stand and stare, craning my neck at the soaring ceiling at least a hundred feet above me and gazing down at the vast floor splashed with color from the jewel-like windows.

Centered directly in front of me, under a single pillar of light, was a statue in glistening white marble—Bridan's "Assumption of Mary." All around me was beauty on a scale that was overwhelming. I wondered that such an edifice could be built at all, considering its size, design, and detail. The fact that it was begun more than twelve hundred years ago and has survived since then is simply awe-inspiring.

The stories that surround this magnificent old church are many. As a matter of fact, the tour guide who was working the day of my visit has written a book about them. Malcolm Miller has been a fixture in Chartres for the past thirty-five years and is widely recognized for the quality of his tours. Hearing him breathe life into the history of the building is to experience storytelling at its best.

Chartres, as an important seat of commerce and social life, dates back until at least the time of the Romans, and it was likely a place of religious significance long before the seventh century, when historical references to the cathedral first began to appear. Over the ensuing few centuries, one might wish that no-smoking policies had been developed in the parish. The cathedral, it seems, was burned down every hundred years or so.

Perhaps the most noteworthy of these catastrophes was the fire of 1194, when it was assumed that the *sancta camisia* was lost. This holy relic, believed to be the wrap worn by Mary when she gave birth to Christ, had attracted pilgrims to the area for centuries, and all Christendom mourned its demise. It turned out, however, that the cloth had survived the fire, hidden away by priests in the cathedral crypt until the fire burned itself out. The miracle of the cloth's resurrection inspired the construction of a new grand cathedral and resulted in the soaring Gothic structure we currently see. The *sancta camisia* remains safely in the cathedral treasury even today.

The eleventh and twelfth centuries seem to have been the turning point for Chartres. About that time, fire was replaced by war as the primary threat to the cathedral's integrity. Chartres was targeted or pillaged during the Hundred Years' War, the French Revolution, World War I, and World War II—to name just the major conflicts that were waged about its grounds. But though all this upheaval, the cathedral building has remained intact. Even the stained glass is original, having been removed to safety by concerned townsfolk during turbulent times.

The cathedral, however, was not completely spared the blood of battle. Dad recollected a story of a sniper who used the church towers as a vantage point to shoot American targets. The gunman had lodged himself behind the cathedral's filigree to provide cover and had proceeded to shoot American soldiers as they ran about the plaza. A GI picked up a bazooka and aimed it at the delicate tower, but he was promptly tackled by an American officer who did not want this sacred landmark defaced in any way. And so this amazing edifice survived once again.

The sniper, who turned out to be a woman, fared much worse. After capture, she was presented to the colonel in command, a man of Jewish background. The sniper promptly spat upon the officer and uttered a derogatory expletive. The colonel fended off requests for a summary execution and simply had the woman confined with other prisoners being debarked for POW camps. An example of the poignant contrasts of hate and mercy engendered by the circumstances of war.

Those who find it difficult to believe in modern-day miracles, need only consider the history of this inspiring old church. After more than eight hundred years of violent human history, this labor of love is still reaching its towers toward the heavens. Surely its preservation is evidence of God's hand.

After about an hour of wandering the cathedral's halls and sanctuaries, I headed back out onto the streets of Chartres. I had no real destination in mind, but since I would eventually have to find Dad and Thom again, I decided I should walk in the general direction of the canals.

The area surrounding the cathedral is quaint and quiet, a pleasant escape from the bustle of a larger city. I had become quite lost in my own thoughts, not to mention the meanderings of the narrow cobblestone streets, when the avenue ended abruptly. In front of me

a narrow stone stairway curved its way sharply up toward a sum-
mit that was beyond my ability to see.

Having no desire to retrace my path, and feeling that the stairs
in front of me must have been designed for pedestrian traffic, I
started up. The steps would have to take me someplace!

Where they took me was to a closed and locked gate set in the
middle of a six-foot, tile-capped, white stucco wall. Now my way
was fully blocked; I had no choice but to go back the way I had come.

As I turned to walk back down the stairs, I heard a low but highly
menacing growl. In front of me and slightly to my left, in a small
alcove off the stairway that I hadn't noticed on my way up, was a dog.

The dog was not of any one particular breed but was definitely
of one particular size: large. It also seemed to be of one particular
disposition—mean—and one particular state of being—hungry!

Images began flashing in my mind, the most vivid being an old
Warner Brother cartoon I used to watch as a kid. A couple of the
characters are stranded in an isolated cabin or a desert island. Food
supplies would dwindle. And then would come the point where Bugs
Bunny or Daffy Duck, delirious with hunger, would start to see his
companion as a succulent roasted turkey.

There is no doubt in my mind that dog was looking at me and
seeing roasted goose.

I backed up a step or two to the gate I had just tried and rattled
its handle again. It did not budge. Now I was stuck. I couldn't go
back; I couldn't go forward.

I tried shouting and lunging toward the animal, but he would not
move except to rear up at my approach and growl more passionately.
He didn't come up after me, though. That dog seemed entirely content to hold me there until I died of natural causes and then to eat me
at his leisure.

The impasse lasted about twenty minutes. At that point I began
to look at the situation differently.

It is amazing, actually, how desperation will lead one to make new assessments. A foolhardy risk will, in a flash, become an obvious and easy solution. I began to think that if I jumped just right, I should be able to swing myself to the top of the wall and lower myself down the other side. My three knee operations suddenly were not a hindrance. The fact I did not know what was beyond the wall was not an issue. The fact that I would have to turn my back on my canine companion was not a problem. It would work—I knew it would.

It might be noted at this point that this was not my first attempted escape from a dog. Thom and I both spent a good deal of our late childhood and early teen years doing just that. In order to survive as paper boys, we had to master the techniques of dog diversion and avoidance.

One dog, in particular, honed our respective skills into an art. Part Dalmatian, part Doberman, part pit bull, and fully possessed by evil, "Spotty" was determined to bring our young lives to an untimely end. He was owned by a timid, gray-haired old lady who seemed to have no problem managing him in the confines of her house. But outside on the street or in her yard, Spotty paid no attention to her reprimands. In the great outdoors, Spotty was in control and he knew it. We knew it too. Tears of fear would spring in our eyes as we approached her door to collect her monthly paper bill.

The dreaded words, "I'll get your money dear. Why don't you play with Spotty while I go to find it?" still echoes in my ears. She would *always* come back and find Spotty chasing me madly up and down in front of her house or snapping wildly at the tendons in my feet as I dangled screaming from a tree above him. Then, invariably, she would coo, "Look at him. He's just a big cute clown!" while I grabbed the money from her hand and fled down her walkway.

Somehow, though, I always managed to escape those jaws of death. And I guess "once a paper boy, always a paper boy." The hound of hades I faced in Chartres didn't get me, either. He leaped as I did and barely missed my left calf, but I made the wall.

If you're out there, Spotty, I'm still alive!

It was fortunate, however, that I did not fling myself all the way over the wall to the other side. The ground was not there, or at least it wasn't immediately available. The other side of the wall dropped off about thirty feet, and the now understandably locked gate opened onto nothing. Any stairway that might once have led down from it had long since been removed.

In sum, I had moved from facing a snarling dog with my back against a wall to straddling a wall with a dog barking wildly below me on one side and a dangerous drop on the other. I was a bit unclear as to whether I had made any progress.

My salvation came in the form of a tiled, inclined roof just off the wall, about thirty feet in front of me. I scooted myself toward it with only minimal abrasions to my person and climbed onto it without much difficulty. Sliding down to the roof edge, I swung myself over and dropped into the street−front table area of a small café.

I did not fully understand the French that was spoken at my appearance. The owner may have told me that he recognized me as one of "the roof−tile stealing Kinkades," or it may have been that he simply wished to serve me eggs and ketchup for brunch. In either case, I waved off the Frenchman's excited speech and trotted down the road in search of my father and brother.

I found them sitting peacefully canalside. Thom was just finish−ing his work.

"Ready to leave for Paris?" he asked.

"I think we had better," I grimaced.

Thom smiled in an understanding way and signed his work.

Cry, "Havoc!"
and let slip the dogs of war.

WILLIAM SHAKESPEARE
Julius Caesar

XII

The Liberation of Paris

I HAVE BEEN TO PARIS TWICE IN MY LIFETIME.
Most unusually for me, I want to go back.

I am not one who likes to repeat adventures. In a world full of experiences, I have always felt there is simply too much to see and do to retrace steps that have already been taken.

Paris, however, is an exception. No one who has ever walked its streets can leave the city without a strong desire to walk them again. Very few people in the world, in fact, are immune to its allure—even those who have not yet visited. Paris is a place where people discover a destiny by finding themselves. And if it is not an individual journey of discovery they desire, perhaps the romance of the city and its culture will help them find someone with which to share a future.

Of course, the first thing they have to do is find a place to park.

As we approached Paris, the traffic began to intensify. At one point we were confronted with stop-and-go conditions. It seemed so out of place to be in the equivalent of L.A. traffic—all those tiny little cars, bumper to bumper—and not a single car stereo was blaring at us. The traffic eventually cleared, and we managed to find our way to the ring road, which took us to the Pont Neuf exit. From there, we drove along the Seine and into the historic district. It took us a while to situate ourselves, and we were confused several times by signs that directed us toward a phantom parking lot that apparently didn't exist. Street parking was out of the question, since every single space seems to fill the second another car leaves. I think a good portion of the traffic on Paris streets is simply people circling, perpetually looking for a parking space.

We finally saw a sign pointing to an underground structure and ended up in a comfortable garage below the streets of Paris. We weren't sure whether we had to pay ahead of time or whether it was the procedure to simply leave the ticket on the dashboard. Nonetheless, we did what we thought was right and left the ticket visible before locking the car and heading out.

We had only a single afternoon and evening to spend in this many faceted city, and I chose to focus my few hours on the experiences that truly epitomize Paris.

To some, this might mean contemplating the timeless art in the Louvre or experiencing the unparalleled view from the Eiffel Tower. But when I think of Paris, the two words that immediately come to my mind are *lingerie* and *guillotines*. So I left Dad to wander the banks of the Seine and Thom to find the quintessential view of Notre Dame while I set out to hunt for these two Parisian essentials, although not necessarily in the same places.

It has become a tradition and a responsibility of any traveler to bring back a token of the places visited to those who have been left behind. For me, this means that I need to shop for a wife and two young sons. The boys, of course, are never really a problem. The world seems geared toward providing the displaced parent with baubles to excite the child waiting at home. But with spouses, things are a bit more difficult.

My wife, Laura, for example, has come home from her last two trips away with a gift of socks. And while it is true that I can always use an extra pair of socks, I think the selection spoke more of a desperate lack of choices than the careful consideration of abundant options. I, it must be said, have not fared much better. One can, after all, only wear so many t-shirts at any one time.

Paris, however, is different. After all, it's the city of romance, the perfect resource for helping a man display his *amour* to the woman in his life. Perfumes, chocolates, and lingerie fill half the shop windows.

I just had to choose the right combination of the three to make my declaration of love to my wife.

Those who might think the silk teddy I purchased is more of a gift to myself than to Laura have never gone through the pain and embarrassment a guy feels in this type of purchase. Being a survivor of several of these endeavors, I now recognize a certain universal pattern in the male efforts expended in this direction. Let me elaborate.

Upon his approach to an "intimate apparel" shop, a solitary man will first scan the other patrons from the outside. He is looking for another male, perhaps someone who has been forced inside by a wife or girlfriend. Barring the observation of such an ice breaker, the potential lingerie customer will then go into a holding pattern, circling the front of the store. He cannot go in alone. The prospect of being isolated in the store without a significant other or at least another empathetic male can create such insecurity that he may withdraw completely. He feels he will be thought of as something akin to a Central Park flasher and fears he will be asked something completely mystifying like, "Does she prefer underwire support?"

If no other male is present inside a lingerie store, men can begin to stack up outside much like airplanes waiting for landing approval. Eventually, however, one guy will be corralled in by a woman, or perhaps an exceptionally courageous customer may even decide to take the plunge alone. Then everyone else will pour inside like water from a broken dam.

Once inside, however, the solo male's troubles aren't over. As intriguing as he might find the merchandise, he cannot bring himself to look at it closely. Again, the fear that he will be arrested on decency charges is rattling about in the back of his mind. Finally, a garment catches his eye. He makes a desperate grab for it, carries it to the clerk, and pulls out his wallet—all without making eye contact with a single person—and dives back out the door. Only after the store is a block or so behind him will he stop, check his wallet to see

Notre Dame, Paris

how much he paid, look at the garment in the bag to make sure it was the right size, and begin breathing again.

"She is sure to love this," he thinks as he heads home with a garment that is an amalgamation of crimson silk, faux leopard skin, and black fishnet.

All these scenarios were running through my mind as I made my approach to a Paris lingerie shop. Nervously I peered past the dainty items in the window to the interior. I was in luck; there was another male already in the store. I could head directly in.

I opened the door and walked to a rack off to the side and toward the back of the store. I thought I could hide there until I got my bearings. I was wrong. I am sure it took less than a minute before the first saleswoman approached. She began addressing me in very excited French about a topic of which I am still uncertain.

When I expressed my confusion in English, the French-speaking clerk called a colleague to help in the translation. Her English was much better than my French, but that is not to say we could actually communicate. From what I gathered, however, both she and the woman I first encountered were intent on showing me everything in the store and on soliciting my opinion about everything they showed.

The glances from other shoppers turned to stares after about ten minutes of this commotion—and I began thinking that I should just hand over my credit card, buy everything, and run.

I was only able to stifle my panic and end the process by exclaiming that the last garment they had shown me was "perfect" and by begging them to "bag it." When I did this, the sales ladies demonstrated their approval by showing the item to several other workers as I followed them across the store to the register. What was supposed to be an stealthy operation had turned into a parade—I still cringe when I think of the ordeal. But as I left the store to the waves of the sales staff, I was already thinking, "She is sure to love this."

If you want to lose your head in Paris, the Palais de Justice is the obvious place to start. This court building, which has been in operation since the thirteenth century, boasts an extremely colorful history and offers some very odd circumstances for the present–day visitor to experience. I wandered in and out of several courtrooms where trials were in session and enjoyed the spectacle immensely.

The lawyers of the French court wear the robes more typically associated with the British courts (although *sans* wigs), and they display a true flair for the dramatic. I do not understand French, and know very little about the country's rules of jurisprudence, but everything that was said in these courts was punctuated with such wild hand gestures and such vocal indignation that these barriers to my understanding were more or less transcended.

It was much like watching an old eight–millimeter home movie in which everyone filmed seems to be on caffeine overload. Fast motions, jittery eye movement, and open–mouthed argument accompanied every point and counterpoint. Although I have absolutely no idea what the trials were about, I was truly entertained. It might also be important to bear in mind, however, that I have a fascination with watching subtitled Kung–fu movies in the original Chinese and occasionally will watch Spanish–language television just to observe the cultural differences.

I hadn't come to the Palais de Justice to simply watch trials, however; I was on my way to the Conciergerie, one of the most infamous prisons in France. I had understood that the old fortress was just around the corner from the court building, but now I was having immense difficulty locating it. Perhaps my pronunciation of the French word *Conciergerie* was less than perfect; at any rate, the guards posted around the Palais seemed at a loss to guide me. I was finally pointed in the right direction only because they recognized the word *guillotine*— and that only when I started making a slicing motion across my neck.

Originally built as a palace, the old prison was converted during the French Revolution and held many prominent figures, including

Maximilien de Robespierre and Queen Marie Antoinette. The actual cells where these two were held are still available for public view. But for me the real attraction of the Conciergerie was the Tour Bonbec, roughly translated as "The Tower of Babble." This structure within the larger prison complex was the site for the court's torture chambers, where confessions were extracted and "justice" imposed by the French Revolutionary Tribunal. In addition to the tower, you can see an actual guillotine, last used in the 1800s, and the Cour des Femmes, a small area set aside for those about to be beheaded to meet with loved ones.

The French have long since done away with the guillotine, viewing it as cruel and archaic. They do, however, retain the right to induce severe indigestion by serving heavy sauces on meat entrees. Americans, on the other hand, will eat only ketchup or perhaps steak sauce on their meat, but hanging is still a government-sanctioned form of capital punishment in two states. In this light, one can easily discern the differences between the two cultures, or at least be reminded to eat lightly before one's own execution.

Or such were the thoughts of one confused traveler after several frantic days on the road.

I left the Palais and wandered down the Ile de la Cite, the river island that is home for both the courts I had just left and the Cathedral de Notre Dame de Paris, where I was heading. The walk down this small bit of land afforded excellent opportunity to enjoy the people watching for which Paris is famous. Both the fashionable and the fashion-impaired seem drawn to this area. This is probably because, as tradition and location would dictate, the island is the heart of Paris. In fact "Kilometer Zero," a sundial set into the ground in front of Notre Dame, is the point from which all distances in France are measured.

The cathedral itself is a grand building but not nearly as spectacular as the one at Chartres. Like most grand European cathedrals, the building is a patchwork of architectural styles, the result of ongoing construction over several centuries. Unlike Chartres, however, the visible architecture suggests this, even to the untrained eye. This is not to say that there are not spectacular elements to be individually appreciated, nor does it suggest that the overall effect is anything

NOTRE DAME, PARIS

but sublime. It does suggest, however, that Notre Dame's most special qualities are not derived from the building itself.

Walking through the Portail du Judgment, I was immediately struck by this realization. This entryway, one of the most famous sights that the cathedral can boast, depicts a dramatic scene of the punishment of sinners and the ascension of the saved into heaven. Yet for all the visual impact of this finely chiseled relief, I was touched more powerfully by what I experienced as I entered. I discovered that it is the congregation of people, the spirit that fills the vessel of the building, that gives this cathedral its power and its mystique.

It was late in the day when I arrived, moving toward the time that the cathedral's galleries would be closed to the general public. Notre Dame's congregation was moving in to reclaim the building from the tourist trade, and its choir was at practice. The sound simply stunned my senses and filled my heart.

Like many men, I have made a lifestyle out of stoicism, of not showing the emotions that have often been roiling inside me. In this case, I sat and I listened and, very unexpectedly, I cried.

It occurred to me later that, in my own spiritual development, I have only rarely been confronted with the truly sacred or the absolutely divine. In that cathedral, on that day, in those voices, I felt the resonance of God.

I could not leave Notre Dame without wandering up the tower staircase to view the city a la Quasimodo. The climb was steep and somewhat claustrophobic, but the perch where I emerged offered a grand panorama of the city and an opportunity to inspect some of the cathedral's ornamental gargoyles closely. To my credit, I did manage to suppress the urge to shout "sanctuary" and to scramble about hunched over.

I descended the steps again, emerged back into the sunshine, and walked off to find the spot where Thom was painting.

I found him on the back side of the cathedral, along the south bank of the Seine. He was ceremoniously chewing his Norman

Rockwell pipe, attracting a crowd, and as typical, eyeing a nearly completed canvas.

"Did you find what you were looking for?" he asked as I approached.

I answered that I had, although I am not fully sure to what Thom was referring.

"Hungry?" he asked.

I shrugged. But Thom is my brother. He knows that I am usually able to eat without much consideration as to whether I actually want or need the food.

"Why don't you go and see if you can find us a pizza?" he continued.

Parisian Pizza? I wondered. "Sure," I said.

My search took me up and down a few of the nearby side streets, but did not take long. I found a small Italian place willing to serve take-out.

The language barrier here was not nearly as problematic as it had been over the previous couple of days. The waiter spoke English to the extent that I felt certain he understood the concept of "pizza with everything." And, because it seemed the thing to do, I ordered a bottle of inexpensive red wine to go with it. He called my order down the shaft of a dumbwaiter, and about ten minutes later the customary pizza box appeared. Smiling broadly, the waiter handed it to me along with the bagged bottle. With several slaps to the back and numerous exclamations of "Enjoy, eh!," I was ushered back out onto the street.

I must admit I felt very pleased that I had accomplished what I had actually set out to do in so little time. I was smiling as broadly as my waiter by the time I returned to my brother.

Situating myself next to Thom, I opened the box, expecting to dole out a few pieces of our snack before opening the wine. And I would have done just that—had the pizza been sliced. Did they want us to fold it into a giant "taco" for consumption? The oddities of this repast did not, however, stop with the impracticality of its serving.

The pizza also had three large uncooked eggs lying "sunny side up" on top of and oozing about its other toppings. I am not sure if I ordered this topping by saying "with everything" or if this is just a standard ingredient in French pizza. I did, however, make a mental note to say, "Hold the raw egg" on my next order.

Thom, getting up from his easel, walked over to the pizza, looked at what I had brought back, and did not hesitate. Cutting a piece with a knife he keeps in his pocket, Thom folded the pizza over on top of itself and took a bite.

"Not bad," he commented as he walked back toward his painting. Though Thom is not a big fan of wine, I was concerned that the light Chianti was the right choice for pizza with eggs.

I can say with both pride and embarrassment that when we were bachelors Thom and I had eaten things that the average person would find disturbing. There was, in other words, never any doubt that the pizza would be consumed; it was just a question of approach. My brother defined what seemed to be an adequate style of intake, and so I cut my own piece, folded it, and ate. Thom was right; it wasn't bad—a little slimy, perhaps, but satisfying.

We had eaten everything but the cardboard box in which the pizza had come when we were joined by a couple of new onlookers who stared intently at Thom's work. It took about ten minutes, but the offer eventually came, "Can I buy your painting? How much do you want for it?"

This has happened before. In Rosarito, Mexico, Thom was painting a luminous sunset over a series of tar-paper shanties that stood on a cliff above a local beach. An owner of one of the shacks, an elderly man, approached and made an offer—roughly the equivalent of twenty dollars of American money. The old gentleman did not, however, stop with the offer of pesos. "I will hang it in the place of honor above my table," he suggested, hoping the chance at immortality would tempt my brother.

Thom was touched by the old man's offer, but he respectfully declined, telling the old man that he never sold anything without Nanette seeing it first. Thom also asked the old gentlemen to sit and talk while he continued to paint. He, Thom, and I spent the next hour in comfortable and friendly conversation.

THE EASEL   PARIS...

On this Parisian street, the offer was no less sincere though much richer than the one made on the Mexican beach. Thom's response, however, was identical. My brother declined but offered conversation.

It was getting late, Thom still had a few things he wanted to clean up on his canvas, and Dad had to be rounded up so we could decide what we should do on our night out in Paris. Thom had arranged to meet Dad at a set time and place and asked if I would be willing to keep the appointment at Pont Neuf, a bridge crossing the Seine, directly down from where he was painting. I agreed and set out down the river bank at a slow trot.

I arrived at the Pont Neuf at the time Thom had specified but with no father in sight. This did not really surprise me; confused times and meeting spots are a tradition of travel with the Clan Kinkade. After a few minutes of consideration, it came to me that the next most logical place for my father to wait might be at the car. As it turned out, I was right. I found Dad leaning against the hood, talking to a garage attendant.

Extricating Dad from this conversation, I walked him back to the street where I had left Thom. I was now concerned that Thom would begin to wonder where we were since we had taken so much longer than expected. This being the case, I decided to run ahead of my father to let Thom know that everything was all right. I asked Dad to continue straight down the street on which we were walking so Thom and I could pick him up on our way back. He assured me that I could go on ahead, that nothing would move him off the street. So I ran on.

I found my brother where I had left him. As he packed his easel, I explained the reason for my tardiness. "At least you found him," Thom said.

We set off back the way I had just come, expecting to meet our father. It took our backtracking all the way to the point where I had left Dad to realize we had lost him again. In this area of Paris, there were no cross-streets to turn off along this route; the street ran directly along the bank of the river. In order for us to miss each other, my father would either have had to jump into the Seine or walk back into the city area where the car had been parked. I could not believe that he would have done either.

Thom and I started heading back down the street toward the point where he had painted his canvas, hoping that somehow we had walked past each other without knowing it. No Dad. Quickly calculating how

far Dad could have traveled on his two knee replacements, we decided
to start checking for him a block in from the river. We were starting
to get worried. Neither of us could think of a reason why anyone
would kidnap an American WWII veteran in a baseball cap that said,
"Old Men Need Love Too," but at this point we had to consider all
possibilities. We frantically cut across the four lanes of roadway that
separated us from the other side of the street, hopping the center island
on the way, and walked about halfway back again to where I had originally left my father. We then headed directly into the city. All we could
do was hope and pray he was all right.

We had not gone more than a few steps in this seemingly arbi-
trary new direction when my brother jerked my arm and pointed.
Dad was sitting in a small corner restaurant, eating spaghetti.

I felt relieved, I felt confused, I felt like laughing, I felt my father
was a nut. As we walked in the cafe, Dad looked up as if all was as
it should be, smiled, and waved us over to the table.

"Aaaah, Dad, why are you eating spaghetti?" I asked when we
had reached the table. I could think of nothing else to say.

"Well, Son, I was hungry."

My brother looked at me and smiled. Dad-ism at its finest.

Good Americans,
when they die,
go to Paris.

THOMAS GOLD APPLETON
quoted in Oliver Wendell Holmes,
Autocrat of the Breakfast Table

XIII

The Beginning of the End

IT WAS MY BROTHER'S IDEA.

He may have been inspired by the notion that the artist Henri de Toulouse-Lautrec has history with the establishment. Or he might have been motivated by the reality that its experience is a cultural obligation for an American visiting Paris, just as visiting Billy Bob's might be for a Parisian visiting Fort Worth. Whatever the reason, Thom decided we should all go and see a show at the Moulin Rouge.

This cabaret, of course, scandalized Paris night life in the late nineteenth century with the introduction of the quadrille, a dance which later evolved into the French Can-Can. It also launched the careers of such entertainment notables as Maurice Chevalier and Josephine Baker. And, it had, from what I heard, retained or regained much of its luster up to the present day. I confess the idea of going intrigued me.

We were dropped off under the famous windmill marquee and into the midst of a throng of people attempting to gain admittance to the show. Given the size of the crowd, it came as a surprise that Thom managed to get us in the building. Doing his best Sinatra imitation, he began tipping everyone who came within reach, and suddenly we were being seated. It was apparent that although money cannot buy happiness, it can buy the staff of the Moulin Rouge.

The show came with a very nondescript dinner and a bottle of inexpensive French champagne. My father, still full of spaghetti, talked while my brother and I ate. Sipping the bubbly hesitatingly, he spoke of his war experiences in Paris and in Brussels. . . .

---◇---

From Chartres my father had been transferred to the small town of Cambrai, about two hundred miles north of Paris on the Belgian border. This did not, however, stop him from participating in the liberation of Paris. He, in fact, had no choice in the matter. Along with many other American soldiers, he was ordered to the city to serve as an "escort" to the returning French army.

Dad was very confused by this order. It seemed that it should be unnecessary to provide support for an army returning as conquering heroes. As it turned out, the number of kisses being forced on the marching Frenchmen were so great that every able-bodied American was needed to appease the grateful onlookers. Had Dad been able to find a place to stay during his time in Paris, he might have thought of this visit as a silver lining for his storm-cloud experiences during the war. Alas, he had no money, and no living arrangements could be procured. He spent his evenings in the "blacked out" Paris streets and slept on a bench in a park.

Upon his return to Cambrai, my father was assigned various duties in and about the city. He worked in the military police and as a transport driver moving materials and personnel back and forth across the Belgian border. Both jobs had their dangers and difficulties. From some of Dad's descriptions, I feel that a certain degree of divine intervention must have been at work to allow for his survival. Even so, and as might be anticipated considering that we are talking about my dad, the dangers came from unexpected sources and from odd directions.

The German army, of course, was still about. Cambrai was shelled several times during my father's stay, and Dad told of an instance when he captured a German spy who had parachuted into the city's perimeter. The infiltrator was dressed as a Polish army regular and was walking about the city claiming to be lost.

Dad does not claim to be a master counter-intelligence officer, but it did seem obvious to him that a Polish soldier was a bit out of place in the north of France. He arrested the man and, to the sound of Polish cursing, placed him in "the tombs," a massive underground vault that was serving as the Cambrai city jail. This cavernous room was lit only by a fifteen-watt bulb and was impossible to navigate without a flashlight. The darkness and the problems of carrying both a pistol and a light while guiding the prisoner apparently left my father open to attack. The fight did not last long, and Dad eventually wrestled his attacker into a cell, not without a receiving a few bumps himself.

Dad's run-in with the spy, however, was not nearly as treacherous as the problems he ran into with other American servicemen. As a member of the military police, my dad had to deal with the disturbances caused by soldiers who got out hand in their off-duty hours. Such situations were not only common, but often quite dangerous due to the deadly mix of testosterone, alcohol, boredom, and high-powered weaponry. In other words, Cambrai was sort of like our childhood hometown on any given Saturday night.

Dad described quite vividly the feeling of being shot at by a drunk artillery man who was certain my father was the enemy. Dad did not want to have to shoot the soldier in order to get close enough to point out his misjudgment. Luckily, the shooter became distracted with the movement of a different police officer, and Dad had opportunity to run up from behind and wrest his weapon away. This American soldier was given ample to time to learn Polish from a German in the underground French jail.

This pattern and type of behavior reached its pinnacle during the Christmas of 1944. The commander stationed at Cambrai took it upon himself to provide everyone under his command with a traditional Christmas feast. As translated by a United States Army officer, this meant that each of his men would receive a pack of cigarettes *and* a bottle of "liberated" champagne. In relatively short order the entire bivouac, except for those on duty, came under the combined influences of alcohol and nicotine.

Sometime during the evening, several of the intoxicated soldiers decided it would be appropriate to climb up to the top of a three-story building. The slick tile roof was slanted steeply, basically the equivalent of an amusement-park superslide. One soldier slipped and was left dangling from the roof. His comrades in arms, of course, immediately expressed their concern by cheering his plight and taking aim at the wriggling target with various small arms.

The Cambrai fire department eventually arrived to pull the unfortunate off the gutter from which he was hanging. Dad took the dangler and several of his buddies to visit with the spy and the artillery man for the remainder of the evening. There was now a full class of students for the Polish language lessons.

As had been the case throughout his military career, the greatest threat to Dad's safety in Cambrai came from neither the Germans or the American military, but from himself. It was sunset, it seems, and Dad was driving a jeep into Brussels on a delivery. Cresting the top of a small hill that lay along his route, he found himself face to face with a German tank. He does not remember how he managed it precisely, but his next memory is of heading back the way he had come at an accelerated rate. Although this, to my mind, was a good direction to be heading and a good decision to make, he lost control of the jeep, and it slid off the road into a ditch. This led to what I consider a bad decision. Jumping from his seat, Dad attempted to pick the vehicle up and set it back on the road.

Now, if Thom and I are any indication, I am sure than my father in his prime was a formidable specimen of manhood. An army jeep, however, weighs in at about a ton, and my father was not equal to the task. My father barely managed to make it back to Cambrai, where he was shipped immediately to an army hospital in Saint-

Quentin for hernia surgery. Luckily for Dad, the German tank operators must have found the spectacle of a herniated American soldier limping home so pathetic that they never opened fire.

The extent of this injury did not stop with my father's operation. The twenty-one-day hospitalization also separated Dad from his most recent lady love. Her name was Bruna Ferrerno, and she was, according to Dad, a beauty as well as a minor countess from Italy. So distraught was Bruna at this separation that she left Cambrai in search of my father and was last seen by Dad's friends "heading north." I assume she found another soldier along the way to soothe her shattered emotions.

My father was so distraught at being away from Bruna that he immediately fell in love with his nurse at the hospital, Clair Wurst. This relationship was something of a problem for Dad in that she was an officer and he was just a lowly enlisted man. The army of that time would tolerate many things, but fraternization of this sort was not one of them.

The two saw each other clandestinely for the period of Dad's recovery and up until Clair was transferred. When she was gone, my father again became distraught. Like Bruna, he set out to find his lost love. Unlike Bruna, he did actually manage to locate the person he was seeking. Clair was in Rheims, France.

They had but one more evening together. They spent it walking, talking, and enjoying the night air until an unfortunate ten-o'clock curfew in the city and an irate police officer ended the date. The only reason they were not arrested was that Clair convinced the officer that Dad was her patient and she was simply attending to him. The officer, nonetheless, escorted them back to the hospital.

My father left the next morning for his company command at Cambrai and an immediate transfer to Liïge, Belgium. He never saw or heard from Clair again.

A broken heart may have been the last injury my father received in war.

Thom, Dad, and I toasted the evening and settled back into our chairs; the show was about to begin. Since the early eighties the Moulin Rouge has produced nine shows, each entitled with a single word that provides an image of what was in store for those in attendance. From reasons unknown to me, each of these single word titles has began with an "F." Two of the earlier shows, for example, were called "Fantastic!" and "Festival!" The revue we were attending was called "Formidable!"

The show was an odd mix of drama and dancing girls, occasionally punctuated by breathtaking novelty acts. One performer set loose a flock of pigeons with miniature lights on their backs. The birds flew around the darkened room for a minute or two, creating an effect somewhat like fireworks. The audience, though thrilled by the sight, still covered their heads and drinking glasses during this portion of the show. At a tweet from the trainer's whistle, the birds flew back to the stage and roosted on a steel grid that spelled the word *merci* in bird lights.

Another performer stunned the crowd by riding a motorcycle down the aisle while doing a wheel stand. A 250CC motor roaring at full throttle in an enclosed room is thrilling enough, but the ensuing stunts were even more amazing. Small jumps were performed in the orchestra pit and then a large plastic ball was brought out by girls in leather biker's costumes. The rider skillfully guided his vehicle into the ball and proceeded to do loop-de-loops in its interior.

The rider then exited the ball and stood beside the still running motorcycle. On making his bow before the cheering audience, though, he clumsily lost control of the cycle, which crashed loudly on the stage and began to turn circles on its side under its own power. The motor sputtered to a halt, and it was some minutes before the rider, after several awkward attempts, managed to kick the bike to life again. To lessen the embarrassment of this mishap, a bevy of Can-Can girls in ruffled skirts began to fill the stage in two rows.

Ste. Michel, Paris

The rider, in a final dramatic stunt, ran the guantlet of ruffles while standing on the seat of the bike and performing another wheelie.

Thom and I were transfixed. As boys on our paper route, the idea of performing wheelies on a motorcycle while riding through crowds of beautiful women would have seemed an ideal career choice.

As the show ended, we faced a long night of driving in our attempt to make it to Brussels before turning in for the night. As it was almost midnight, this seemed a long shot but, never to be daunted, we decided to try anyway. The cabbie on the drive back to our car made an attempt at interesting us in yet another local place of entertainment.

It is amazing how many euphemisms are used for the obvious. The driver constantly referred to the "fine entertainments" which were available and also mentioned the "superb accommodations" one could find there if a gentleman were generous. He claimed their service was of "the most excellent variety" and further professed that the girls at the "cabaret" in question were college students who simply worked there as a means of earning extra money for school. They were, of course, the most beautiful girls in all of Paris, being so young and innocent. We couldn't help but raise our eyebrows at this last description.

When he could see he was failing to get our interest, the route back to our parking lot became much more direct.

On the drive to Brussels, Thom and I had a rather lively discussion. What started simply enough on the subject of gun control evolved into a general philosophical discussion of the relative merits, successes, and failures of various political policies.

Throughout our discussion, Dad was asleep in the back seat, although his ears did perk up when Thom proceeded to question the political effectiveness of Franklin Delano Roosevelt's "New Deal." At that point, Dad shot bolt upright and said impatiently, "How can

GROTE
MARKT
BRUSSELS

I sleep back here when someone's knockin' tar out of FDR?" Spoken like a true WWII veteran.

We arrived in Brussels very late. The last part of the trip had been one of those where you talk about anything to help keep the driver awake and continually fear that you will glance over to see that the look of concentration you thought was guiding the car down the road was mild catatonia. Considering the intensity of the previous two days, I am not sure how Thom managed to stay awake at all. The hotel's bed was exceptionally comfortable that night, and I welcomed sleep.

We awoke the next morning in Brussels with no clear objective in mind. On a whim, I suggested that we visit the town square, the Grote Markt (or "Grand Place") which I had heard was very beautiful.

The church, the town hall, and the many romantically named guild halls that form the perimeter of the Grote Markt are architecturally spectacular. Multicolored hanging flags and a central flower market add vivid splashes of color to complement the intricately detailed facades. Victor Hugo claimed this space to be the "most beautiful" forum in the world during his stay there in De Duif, "The Dove," a house on the square.

As a bonus, the Grote Markt proved an ideal spot for people watching. The mixture of locals and tourists milling about the area provided a strong sense that this was a true crossroads, a place where all travelers will eventually find themselves.

Thom, Dad, and I took advantage of the markets in and about the square to shop for small tokens for our respective families and to commemorate the impending end of our journey. Thom found a set of antique candleholders perfect for the entryway of his home; he was sure Nanette would be pleased with the purchase. I became immediately taken with a small pen-and-ink drawing being offered by a gypsy artist named Jean Lebec. He called it "The Embrace."

The artist, whether by circumstance or design, seemed truly haunted by this work, telling me it represented "a special moment in his life." Since that time, Jean claimed, he had fallen into despair, living in the open and eking out a day-to-day living off the sales of his work. "Alienation and isolation" were, he suggested, his only companions on his journey. I, however, suspect the artist also met up with and embraced an ale or two along his way. Whatever the truth of the matter, I bought the piece, listened to his story, and hoped that Laura would appreciate the purchase.

Dad did not find any anything special to buy. He did, however, became quite enamored with a group of Ecuadorian street musicians playing in the square. According to my father, this same band had being playing in Old Town Sacramento the last time he had been there. I found this interesting because I could have sworn that I had watched the group perform in Buenos Aires. To my imagination, the dispersion of these sightings qualifies the group as the Elvis Presleys of the folk-music world—they pop up here and there, only to be sighted somewhere else entirely at a later date.

We separated soon after this serendipitous concert, each pursuing our own interests. Thom, of course, settled into his own world of color, light, and form and produced yet another oil sketch. Dad decided to pay a visit to the Cathedral of Saint Michael. His fascination with churches, I suppose, matches that of many visitors to Europe, but after Chartres and Notre Dame the idea of another such excursion did not really attract me. I decided instead to indulge my taste for kitsch.

For those not familiar with Yiddish, the word *kitsch* refers to art of questionable value or taste. For example, I once visited a statue of the "world's largest jackelope" in my home state of Texas that would qualify as such an exhibit. And just to prove I am not alone in my family as having an interest in these things, I can proudly point out that my sister, Kate, has paid homage to Cadillac Ranch, a series of classic cars buried end up in west Texas. In Brussels, of course, such a palette can only be satisfied by a visit to the Mannekin Pis.

Although I assume that many people would be familiar with the Mannekin Pis by sight, few may recognize the name. The Mannekin Pis is a small bronze statue of a little boy urinating into a fountain. It is described as the "first citizen of Brussels" and as the most popular tourist attraction of the city. Setting aside speculation on whether that last claim might be signaling the end of Western civilization, the experience of seeing the statue was actually quite satisfying. The Mannekin Pis itself, however, was not really the source of the enjoyment. The real attraction is the spectacle surrounding the little statue.

The crowds that make the pilgrimage to see the Mannekin Pis are large, excited, and diverse. They stand staring at the little boy as if to do so will provide an insight into the nature of life that can only be had from the vision. The commentary running through the crowd spans a variety of topics but seems primarily focused on two questions: "Why would that little boy do what he is doing?" and "Who is he, anyway?"

I, like the people around me, considered these questions. Unlike the people around me, however, I thought the answers were quite obvious.

STATUE OF
"MANNEKIN PIS"
BRUSSELS

The answer to the first question can be simply stated but is really quite complex in its psychological and social implications: The Mannekin Pis is doing what he's doing because "it's a guy thing to do." That little boy stands smiling at the passing crowd and relieving himself simply because he can.

It is a sense of empowerment that first strikes all young boys at the dawn of a burgeoning masculinity. "Gee," the boy will think to himself, "I can go anywhere I want." For the rest of his life, the male will relive this initial realization again and again to reassert himself and gain some sense of control in his life. I have two little boys who are just now, as I write these words, recognizing this joy. As a result of this enlightenment, and as Thom and I did before them, my sons are marking a great deal of territory these days.

And that brings me to the obvious answer to the second question, for I have no doubt about the statue's identity. That little boy is, without a doubt, modeled after my boy Nicky. The face, hair, body, and stance are all the image of my youngest son. I am convinced that all the history I have read concerning the casting of the bronze in 1619 by Jeremy Duquesnoy, a well-known artist of the time, are fictions designed to divert the curious from this highly evident truth: My boy is the Mannekin Pis.

Two other circumstances add to the rich yet odd history of this small statue.

Over the many years, it seems, fans of the Mannekin Pis have taken it upon themselves to supply the naked child with clothing. The first of these fashion statements appeared in 1698, and more than 350 others have appeared since that time. The designs of the clothing have ranged from an American jogging suit to a matador's garb and cape.

These suits of clothes always appear on the statue in the dead of night, are placed anonymously, and are enjoyed for a time before they are added to the permanent collection on display nearby at the Broodhuis, a museum dedicated to their preservation. Two of the sets of clothes are, in fact, now placed on the statue as an annual event.

The Mannekin Pis wears a marquis's outfit every year to designate the first day of the annual Brussels's Fair and a Welsh Guard's uniform to honor the Allied liberation of the city on 3 September 1944.

It might be noted that this tradition is, when put in perspective, tantamount to the defacement of a valuable antiquity. The statue is, after all, a four-hundred-year-old casting made by a celebrated artist. One wonders if the Italians would tolerate having boxer shorts slipped on Michelangelo's "David" every now and then in an attempt to provide him wish some modicum of privacy.

Another interesting circumstance is the extremely disturbing commercialism that coincides with the little statue's existence. Along the Eikstraat and the Stoofstraat, the streets that intersect at the Mannekin Pis fountain, shops are filled with replicas of the statue in every size and to fit every taste. Everywhere one looks, there are thousands upon thousands of little boys relieving themselves. Hundreds, moreover, are being purchased and carted about by happy tourists thinking proudly, I presume, that they know the perfect place to display them in their own homes.

This scene reached a crescendo when I wandered up to the "mother" of all Mannekin Pises. This one was eight feet tall and the small stream shot by the original had become a firehose blast in this iteration. I went from being awestruck to frightened to envious—with very little time in between the emotions. If I would have had the means to transport this monstrosity, I might have brought it home to Texas where it might have had a chance of being deemed acceptable. Perhaps the statue would even have found a home beside the world's biggest jackelope.

———————◇———————

It was well into the afternoon when I left the area of the fountain and began looking for Dad and Thom. Walking along the street that leads back to the central square, I noticed that many of those passing me were eating some sort of unfamiliar but delicious-looking pastry. These heavily sugared confections smelled like the best doughnut shop I have ever visited and were roughly the size of a small briefcase. It took a minute, but I came to realize I must be looking at an authentic Belgian waffle.

"Well," my stomach thought to itself, "This is a must eat on a visit to Brussels."

Letting my nose guide my path, I found myself standing in front of the best-stocked pastry shop I had ever seen. The staff of this "waffle-torium" was working at an exhausting pace creating fresh product for the appreciative crowd of purchasers.

Making my way to the counter I communicated my order for a waffle and a "muffin sort of biscuit thing" called a speculoos. This apparently is another type of baked good for which Brussels is known. After eating both, I would say that while the biscuit was exceptionally tasty, the waffle was sublime. (I know I may have damaged my creditability for making such an assessment since I have already admitted to eating burger puffs and egg pizza.) The waffle, along with the churros found in Guadalajara and the beignets found in New Orleans, now belongs in my personal pastry pantheon.

Dad was asleep on the stone steps beside my brother's easel. Thom was feeding the pigeons in the square he had just painted. We woke our father. "You want a Belgium waffle, Dad?" The suggestion seemed to liven him noticeably.

"How you feeling, Dad?"

"Oh, Son, I don't know . . ." he sighed. A week on the road was beginning to take its toll.

Dost thou think,
because thou art virtuous,
there shall be no more
cakes and ale?

WILLIAM SHAKESPEARE
Twelfth Night

XIV

Escape from Liige

WE LEFT BRUSSELS IN THE EARLY EVENING and drove toward Liige, Belgium, the furthest point north where my father was stationed during his European campaign. The town, by most accounts, is strikingly beautiful, nestled at the confluence of two major rivers and skirting the edges of some of the greatest European forests still standing today.

In Dad's memory, however, Liige was something different. It was the point where war lost nobility and became only tragedy, a place where death was real and so was the insanity of the situation that made death a daily event.

In those days, the Battle of the Bulge was raging. Whole cities were being ground to dust by the armies trampling through them. Stories of the front were circulating madly throughout the populace as the war's casualties were being shipped back through the city. At night, V–1 rockets shelled the city. While daytime saw a facade of normalcy return to the citizenry and the soldiers, everyone knew that life was anything but normal.

I do not know what I expected when we returned our father to this place. This was essentially the end of his journey of remembrance, and I supposed it must have a special meaning to him. As a young man Dad had undergone an experience that is only barely comprehensible to my brother and me. In the past few days he had been reliving this time in order to place its impressions and meanings into the time capsules of our minds. It would be our responsibility to carry the learned lessons of the war forward to the next generation.

We were quiet as we drove into the city, perhaps thinking of these weighty issues.

"Well, Dad," Thom commented somewhat expectantly, "where would you like to go first?"

"I don't know," my father replied. "Drive around. Who knows, I might recognize something."

There was a silence.

"You *might* recognize something?" I asked with mild astonishment in my voice. "We've come eight thousand miles from home on the off chance you *might* recognize something?"

"Well, that church looks sort of familiar," he said.

Through the tears of laughter in our eyes, Thom and I could not have felt closer to my dad than at that moment.

Stay what you are Dad. It is enough, and we love you for it.

———————◇———————

My father finally found an old municipal building where he had worked and took a picture of himself in front of it. He also told us a story of a master sergeant who took it upon himself to sell the Liïge airport back to the Belgian government.

Apparently the sergeant had no authorization from any military authority to do so, but a good price was offered by the Belgian officials, and it is hard for an American to pass up a deal. So, the bargain was struck and the handshake that closed the sale is still etched in my father's mind.

With both the reminiscence and the photograph, we ended up spending more time in Liïge than we anticipated.

Our plane was scheduled to leave the next morning from Frankfurt, Germany, a good two hundred miles away. We knew we would need to arrive early to allow time for the inevitable complications of checking in for an international flight.

It wasn't until about eight o'clock that evening that we finally hit the road for Frankfurt, however. And it was about fifteen minutes later that disaster hit.

It has often struck me as odd that car-rental companies will turn a vehicle worth tens of thousands of dollars over to a stranger and then, in effect, tell that person, "For an additional seven dollars a day you won't be liable for anything that happens to the car." The managers of such an enterprise have apparently never stopped to think that such an arrangement is almost a license to kill, that somebody might pay that small price just for the chance to go four-wheeling in a Cadillac.

It is not my intent to suggest that such a thing happened on this trip, but I bring it up because my brother, out of habit, had arranged for such coverage. And, for only the second time in my experience, the expenditure paid off.

Before we left Liïge we stopped to get gas, some road snacks, and directions. Thom hopped out to start the fueling, I wandered into the station to locate Frankfurt on a map, and Dad sat reading in the back of the car. Thom finished, we paid, and we both got back in the car.

We pulled out that station thinking we had beaten the odds. We had run the car and ourselves to the brink of destruction for days and nothing had snapped. Thom and I were still coherent, Dad was still with us, and the car was still running. That satisfaction remained with us for at least a few more miles. We were on the highway and had reached cruising speed when the engine began to stutter, mildly at first, but more severely within minutes. As we drifted on to the road's shoulder, the engine continued to run, but it was providing no power to the wheels. We jerked and rattled to a halt.

Thom sat quietly for a moment and then asked, "What color is the diesel pump handle at home?"

"Green, I think," came my response. Our rental car used diesel.

"Well," he said, "Green must mean unleaded here. Looks like I just filled this diesel car with unleaded."

"C'est la drag," I murmured.

We had just effectively killed our car . . . and our ride to the airport.

Leaving Dad with the car, Thom and I began trotting along the roadway. Our intent was to reach an overpass that we could see in the distance, cross over the traffic flow, make it back into the city outskirts, and find a phone. As it happened, one of God's tender mercies found us first. An older couple, seeing our apparent distress, pulled over to offer us a ride. We gladly accepted. We knew this assistance was nothing short of miraculous. After all, when was the last time you were driving down the freeway at night, saw two disheveled, good-sized men shambling up the road in the darkness, and had the sudden urge to pull over and ask if help was needed.

In very little time found ourselves being dropped off near a gas station at what we perceived to be a pay phone. But although the phone was public and in working order, it did not, as we expected, operate on money; its user had to insert some sort of prepaid phone card. My brother summed this discovery up quite adequately with a single, monotone syllable: "Ouch."

We headed to the gas station in hopes that they would let us use their phone or could provide us with a card so that we could access the public service.

There are many things in life that are easy to take for granted until they are denied you. In that gas station, Thom and I were reminded that a shared language is one of them. Communicating the idea that we wished to use the phone was difficult; expressing our desire to call a taxi was next to impossible; telling the cab company where we were and where we needed to go was insurmountable.

That we ended up in a cab heading back to the car was truly a miraculous event. The saving grace this time occurred when a customer at the station stepped into our situation, explaining our needs to the attendant and our whereabouts to the taxi company. Without his help in translation, we would have very likely ended up buying canned peaches and a mop from a market delivery service.

After retrieving Dad and our belongings, we set about the next task at hand. We had to locate an office of our rental-car company, tell them of the whereabouts of the car we had just abandoned, and hopefully acquire another one so that we could catch our plane. The driver was of no help in this regard. He did not know of any car rental offices, and his dispatcher apparently knew even less. I thought it odd for a taxi service to claim ignorance about the city they were serving, but considering the way things were going up to that point, I shouldn't have been surprised.

After a brief discussion, Thom suggested the airport as a good place to start looking for car-rental agencies. With that as destination we were back on the road.

Though I have referred to Liige as a town, I think the term might have been misleading. Liige is, in fact, a small city with a quarter of a million people. With that population and with the commercial development that surrounds the city, I expected the airport to be of some substance—a view of things that I now recognize as decidedly American.

It was a bad sign when we pulled up to the terminal and the lights were off. We had the driver circle the entire complex, and nobody was to be seen. In fact, the look of this facility went well beyond closed and moved toward abandoned and derelict. I began wondering if the sergeant who had sold the place to the Belgium government had left them the keys to get in!

The state of the airport, however, did give perspective to our situation. There is a rule to traveling that we all knew in our hearts but that we had ignored up until now in our assessment of the situation. Its wisdom was probably most eloquently captured in a statement made by the matron of all travelers, Dorothy, in *The Wizard of Oz*. "Toto," she says with conviction, "I don't think we're in Kansas anymore."

"We'll need someplace to sort this out," Thom suggested.

"Have him take us to a major hotel," I said. "There is bound to be a concierge or somebody at the desk who at least speaks some English." That was a pretty bold assumption in light of our experience with the cab company and the airport.

"Large hotel, help, downtown, big building!" Thom was gesturing with his arms and speaking loudly, hoping it would help the driver learn English. I have never really been sure if loud English is actually some sort of international language, but in this case it got the desired result. After several minutes of blank stares we were off, heading back toward the city.

In light of how the evening was progressing, it would have been far too normal for the drive back into Liïge to occur uninterrupted, so of course a problem arose. We had made it off the highway and onto a surface street when the lights hit us.

There are few things that are fully cross-cultural, but the flash of police car lights is recognizable no matter where you are, and it always means trouble. Our driver began murmuring under his breath as the officer approached. Words were passed through the window, and then the officer removed our driver from the car and walked him toward the storefront by which we were parked. Again, words were passed, this time with a little more heat and with gestures toward the cab. Twice a flashlight traced over the car. The three unshaven faces smiling from the back seat could have done little to instill confidence, and it began to seem that we were being implicated in a major crime of some sort.

"Great," I thought, "we are going to be arrested. They will find out that we broke into Blarney Castle, smuggled fireworks out of Mexico into California, and went four-wheeling in a rented Cadillac. We're doomed." The image of a stay in Turkish prison passed through my mind.

Before I could start screaming for an American consulate, however, the situation abruptly ended. The driver reappeared at his door, climbed in, and pulled back onto the street. I don't know why we were stopped, and the driver could not offer much illumination on the issue.

"No problem!" he offered in his best and only English.

---◇---

The driver did drop us off at a hotel and, by God's grace, we did find a clerk who not only had a command of the English language but was also very willing to help. We, at this point, had three options.

First, we could get another rental car and leave the one we had on the road to be picked up in the morning by the company that owned it. This turned out to be impossible; the closest car agency with an open office was in Frankfurt, which was where we were trying to go in the first place.

Another option was to secure alternative transportation to Frankfurt and, again, simply leave our rental car to be handled by others in the morning. This also turned out not to be possible. The airport was abandoned, and we had missed the last express train to Frankfurt. There was a commuter line which would arrive in Frankfurt an hour before our plane left, but that would leave no time for check-in.

The third choice available did not seem much more promising than the first two, but it was all we had. Thom arranged for a towing service and went in search of a mechanic who would be willing to attempt a repair on our car.

It was now about ten o'clock on Saturday night.

Our plane would be leaving in less than twelve hours from an airport two hundred miles away.

---◇---

Thom was gone. He had left with the towing service in search of what I perceived to be the holy grail of late-night auto repair. Dad and I were left to our own devices, waiting for my brother and the outcome that I knew only he could arrange. It was late, we had not yet had dinner, and so we decided to use our time to that end. We went into the hotel restaurant and got a table, then I left Dad and went to make a phone call to Laura. I wanted to let her know what was happening and warn her that we might have a delay in coming home.

When I returned to the restaurant, I found my father already eating. It was one of those situations where you suddenly realize how long it has been since your last meal, how hungry you are, and that whatever it is that is being dished up is absolutely what you want to eat. In this case Dad had ordered a steak, medium rare, with a side of spaghetti. I coveted that meal.

This, of course, was not a novel sensation to me. Food in general and beef in particular is, if anything, my major vice. I come to this naturally. After all, our clan for several generations has placed a high value on a hearty meal. As kids, our family would make regular pilgrimages to the Mecca of Perry Boy's Smorgy in Sacramento and revel in conspicuous consumption. It was a place where you could eat as much as you wanted, as long as you wanted, and, if you did it right, would leave the establishment in literal pain from gastronomic indulgence. As husky eight- and nine-year-old boys, Thom and I definitely pushed the outer limit of the envelope in relation to the "all you can eat" policy. It got to the point that the management of Perry Boy's would simply shake their heads when they saw the two of us approach. The ninety-nine cent charge for the "children's meal" was certainly a losing proposition for the restaurant in our case.

Thom's specialty at Perry Boy's was flavor experimentation. He would attempt every combination of food he could imagine in search of the perfect taste. "Try it, Pat. Jello with beef gravy. Not bad!" he would say. His work in this regard, though creative, was often only fully appreciated by me.

I, on the other hand, abandoned the novelty of taste testing in favor of setting records for consumption of certain familiar items. Macaroni and cheese was a specialty at this time, usually ingested in portions roughly the equivalent of five percent of my total body

Brussels

weight. Another favorite selection was beef, specifically hamburger. The patties at Perry Boy's were smothered in brown sauce and piled high on the stainless steel trays in a manner resembling rather greasy stacks of over-browned pancakes. I moved quickly past the short stack category and on to the realm of the full stack. To my knowledge, my record of seven patties in one sitting is a Perry Boy's record and was never bested by any boy my age.

I have since moved to Texas and, almost as an obligation, have learned to appreciate beef even more. This is, after all, a state with a restaurant that boasts the "Big Eighty," an eighty-ounce piece of meat so large that if one person eats it all in a single sitting the meal is free. I plan to test that policy some day. As hungry as I was that night in Liège, I would have ordered the "Big Eighty," downed it with the pasta that was being served as a side dish, and looked forward to dessert. But the luck of the night struck again, and this time it was a tragedy that truly hit home.

I quickly scanned down the menu in search of the meal my father had ordered. Almost immediately I came across "Steak American" as a recommended option. To my mind, there was no more apt description of what my father was enjoying—a large, well-marbled piece of beef, simply charred over what must have been a flame broiler. There is nothing more American. I ordered without bothering to confer with my father or attempting a translation of the German which followed "Steak American" as a description of the dish.

My wait for the meal was shorter that I expected. The waiter left and reappeared almost immediately with a small bowl of mayonnaise and a tray of relishes and seasonings. I did not question their appearance, but it did seem a little odd that I was given vinegared cucumber and caper while Dad had steak sauce and ketchup sitting in front of him.

Still, I took comfort in the fact that I had ordered Steak American. There is little that can be done to a piece of meat in its cooking that I could not palate. For example, during my childhood, when money was tight, my mother could make a half–pound of beef stretch into eight hamburgers, enough to feed four. She added so much oatmeal to the meat patty that it practically qualified as a vegetarian meal. And I loved those hamburgers. So, odd condiments or no, I was certain to enjoy this meal.

When the plate was set in front of me, I distinctly remember that the first words out of my mouth were an astonished, "What is it?"

The reply from my waiter before he directed his attentions to the needs of other patrons was a simple, "Steak American."

The next thought in my mind was, "Where in the name of all that is decent do the Europeans get their information about how steak is typically served in America?"

I suppose there are those who would have enjoyed the meal as a gourmet experience, calling it steak tartare. Taking small amounts of the provided garnishes and adding them to the finely ground raw meat, they would have savored the mingling of flavors, using the various provided crackers as vehicles to the palate. To me, my "Steak American" was nothing more nor less than a half pound of uncooked beef mush plopped on a plate and accompanied by saltines.

The people of Belgium had done what I had thought impossible.

They had turned good beef into something almost beyond my capabilities to eat.

The night had turned just about as bad as it could get. The car, the potential of missing our scheduled departure, and now dinner. I wondered how a single six–hour period could have so much misfortune. In between bites of beef spread, I alternated between being tired, frustrated, and worried.

Dad popped the last chunk of his succulent steak in his mouth. While still chewing, he lifted his head and chimed in a familiar comment, "Are we having fun yet, Pattypoo?"

———————◇———————

Thom reappeared after about two hours.

"We're back on the road," he said, smiling. "I found a guy willing to open his shop to flush the tank."

"A-mazing," I pronounced. Things began to look as if they would work out. We were still three or four hours away from Frankfurt, but we had nine hours before the plane left. We would be tired on the flight home, but with ten hours of air time that wouldn't be a problem. A drive, a nap, a wait at the airport, another nap, and we would be home.

—————◇—————

We awoke the next morning at seven o'clock for what was to be our last day in Europe. We had slept only three hours. Although our hotel in Frankfurt was only about fifteen minutes from the airport, we wanted to allot at least two hours for check-in. A quick shower, a few adjustments to our luggage, and we were checking out of our hotel. Thirty minutes later, about an hour before our flight, we were in line for check-in. We thought we had made it.

The time it takes to board an international flight out of Frankfurt is as close as you can get to being caught in a cattle corral with a herd going to slaughter—without actually mooing.

I have been caught in badly delayed check-in lines for most of my married life. My wife, who was born in Mexico and spent three or four days there before moving to the United States, still holds a foreign passport. (For various reasons, her attempts at becoming a naturalized citizen have never seemed to work out.) So while I am afforded the relative status of American documentation, poor Laura is often directed to a line for people who have lost their passport, are carrying weapons, or are traveling with stock animals. I stand with her and so am fully aware of how long a strip search should take.

The lines at Frankfurt were even slower than we had expected. Moving through an initial check-in line took most of the time we had left. Moreover, through a quirk of the line flow, I was separated from Thom and Dad and was moved ahead of them. When I got to the counter to present my ticket, the airline agent suggested that my brother and father leave the line and check in at the gate to avoid missing the flight. I turned over my luggage to the agent, Thom and Dad left the line as suggested, and we all moved as quickly as we could through the airport to our gate.

For one portion of the trip to the gate we were offered a ride on an electric cart with a flashing light on top. Dad was given the seat beside the driver, while Thom and I rode conspicuously on the back tailgate. This afforded us the opportunity to wave courteously as the two of us, both men full of robust health, were shuttled past invalids, senior citizens, and assorted tired, shuffling masses. The overall impression was that two goldbrickers had stolen a ride on the back of a card intended for the handicapped. The absurdity of this predicament caused us both to laugh riotously, but after all, we were in danger of missing our flight and without the cart Dad would never make it on time.

We were beginning to be to be confident we would actually make the flight when we ran into yet another line at the security checkpoint. This delay lasted another twenty-five minutes. After sprinting the last two hundred yards, we arrived at our gate with less than ten minutes until departure.

Thom and Dad approached the woman at the gate to check their luggage. There was a brief conversation punctuated with the most feared words in the vernacular of air travel, "I am sorry, sir. The flight is overbooked."

Hearing these words, the traveler is immediately cast into a sort of Bermuda Triangle for travelers, a Sargasso morass from which there may be no exit. Indeed, it is the uncertainty that makes the statement the more frightening. If you hear "The plane is on fire!" at least you know where you stand. Clearly, the airline did not take the fact you paid a thousand dollars for a ticket as reason to believe you really had the intention of using it. Why should your mere presence at the airport prompt them to actually give you the seat you had reserved three weeks in advance? With overbooking, you could be at the airport wandering forever, the airline dangling a potential for departure just out of arm's reach.

I approached the ticketing agent. "We're traveling together. The agent at the front desk sent us here to check-in. I've already been assigned a seat."

She looked at my boarding pass and flatly stated, "You can go or stay, but there is no room for your friends." Then she added, as if it would make it all seem reasonable, "All the airlines do it. It keeps prices down."

It crossed my mind that if an auto dealer sold the same car to several customers, he too could probably reduce the price of that given vehicle to any single buyer. I doubt, though, the courts would look at it as a protection for the consumer.

I looked at Thom and Dad. I felt that if I went, I would be abandoning them. It would be like Porthos leaving Aramis and D'Artagnan or Curly leaving Larry and Moe. Musketeers or Stooges, it just did not feel right to separate until the trip was truly over. Still, as the agent waited, I felt I could not delay any longer. I had two university classes filled with students eagerly awaiting my arrival in Fort Worth. In less than thirty-six hours, I had to be there. Even worse, I had another plane to catch in San Francisco that would take me to Fort Worth. I had to make that connection in less than twenty hours.

I decided. I hugged Thom and Dad and boarded the plane to begin my flight home alone.

———————◇———————

My father was still stationed in Liège when yet another set of transfer orders came down through the chain of command. This time he was ordered not further into the European theater of war operations, but to the South Pacific. His ship would sail out of Marseilles, France, cross the Mediterranean, then cut through the Suez Canal to the Red Sea and the Indian Ocean. My father and his company were to be part of the invasion of Japan.

Eleven days later, on 6 August 1945, the bombing of Hiroshima and Nagasaki effectively ended the war. My father's orders were canceled, and he was told he could go home.

The victory ship *Woodrow Wilson* brought Dad back to the United States. Stationed at Camp Kilmer in New York, he was given the opportunity to re-enlist and was given forty-five days to make up his mind.

He chose civilian life, although "home" was never the same after the war. Four children, three marriages, ten jobs, thirty-seven automobiles, one million miles on the road, and three Chihuahuas later, he had returned to Europe in hopes of living that part of his life again. And now he *couldn't* get home.

———————◇———————

The plane roared down the runway and lifted into the air with all of the usual sounds of strain. The bumps and moans of air travel should be familiar to me by now, but they invariably set my mind pondering about the absurdity of climbing forty thousand feet in the air inside something so ephemeral as a plane. The seatbelt sign flashed off. Most air disasters happen during take off and landing, so I told myself I'd have another ten hours of life before fate was tempted again.

I was in the middle seat of a "five across" row in the economy section of an overbooked airplane. In other words, I was so cramped that I had to time my breathing with the people on either side of me to allow room for my chest to expand. I could not get up or out easily, and the temperature was beginning to rise. Air travel in these conditions is akin to the "hot box" experiences they used to put prisoners though in POW camps during WWII.

I sat wondering how Thom and Dad were doing. Being psychologically prepared to return home, only to experience a major delay, can undermine the fortitude of even the hardiest traveler. Despite my anticipated ten hours of discomfort, I felt guilty for being here, going home, while they were left behind.

"Yo, Pasch."

If it had been any other word but "Pasch," I would have thought that the voice I heard had been only an uneasy conscience talking. No one uses that name except my brother, and he has called me that since childhood.

I looked up, and Thom was standing smiling in front of me. I was speechless. Another miracle had just materialized before my eyes.

"Comfortable?" he asked, observing my sardined condition.

"How did you did you get on the plane?" I ignored the question about my seating arrangement.

"I kept after them until they finally relented, checked the plane, and found seats for Dad and me."

Things always seem to work out for my brother. Still, I thought, the woman who had informed us of the overbooking had been so final about the lack of seats; they must have opened the cargo hold to fit Dad and Thom on the plane. "Where are you sitting?" I asked.

Thom smiled again. "We're in first class. No extra charge either."

My mouth dropped open, but no words came out.

"I'll drop back later. They're serving brunch now, and then I want to stretch out and get some shut eye." With a wink he was gone.

My brother, I'm telling you, lives right.

I believe each life
is filled with God's miracles;
you only need to look around a bit
and see them.

THOMAS KINKADE

Epilogue

AFTER TEN HOURS OF AIR TIME and two silent movies (my headset didn't work) we landed.

When we set foot in America, I looked at Thom and Dad and knew with great satisfaction that together we had done something few ever have the chance of doing: We had relived history and, in a way, had made a bit of history ourselves.

Thom's driver was waiting for us at the curb. And while we may have been back in the United States when we landed, I knew we were really home when we stopped at a Taco Bell on the way back from the airport. It amazed me that a stretch limousine could fit around a fast-food drive-through, but it did, and we were all soon eating burritos. We later ate a spectacular turkey dinner prepared by Nanette to celebrate our return. It was nice to find the home fires still burning.

My father was the first to leave. We all shook hands and hugged as we had in Frankfurt and promised we would have another travel reunion as soon as time permitted.

"Perhaps Mexico next time," Thom said.

"You'd better believe it!" Dad answered. A heart of adventure will always live in our father.

Then he was off. And I looked after him thinking how important it is to set and follow the right priorities in life. It was a very wise person who pointed out that no one ever lies on his or her deathbed and thinks, "I wish I would have spent more time at work." Our days on this earth are precious beyond any material price. Time should never be spent any way but well.

I think it can also be said that there is no greater use for time

194

than to spend it with the people you love and the people who love you. These are the ones who will carry you with them beyond even your own limited existence and pass you to others beyond theirs. And holding others in your heart, in turn, grants them their own earthly immortality. Family and friends should be celebrated and cherished now, when they are with you and while you are able, or that legacy will pass you by without ever having the chance to flourish.

Only God can guarantee tomorrow.

I don't want to waste a single today.

In the years after the war, my father became active in both the Veterans of Foreign Wars organization and the American Legion. He, in fact, took my brother and me to so many "spaghetti feeds" at "the hall" that we suspected he might have Italian blood. This suspicion was later reinforced when Dad once suggested he might have been adopted as a child and his real parents were possibly a Sicilian couple named Chicarelli who operated a laundry in St. Louis.

That being another story, I'll leave it for another time. My only hope in mentioning these organizations is to suggest that those of you who have access to them should use them for personal discovery. Yes, they may be made up of crusty old men reliving war stories, but you can live each story in their retelling for the first time. We are rapidly losing my father's generation, and all the stories of the war they have to tell will die with them—unless someone listens. It would be a shame to lose the individual experience of such a crucial time in world history. As I write these final words, many things still unsaid fill my mind. My family, like all families, has so much history that I could not record it in a single volume. Moreover, the lessons that might be taken from that history would require even more writing to capture than the simple narrative used to recount it. Thom and I have thought about other trips together: peeling back the tourist veneer and discovering the soul of Mexico; a journey to discover the lands and people that Jesus knew; perhaps even a trek on some high mountain in search of Shangrila.

We may, in other words, meet again.

Roads go ever ever on.

J. R. R. TOLKIEN
The Hobbit

To the Reader

Except for a few name changes and elaborations, all of what I have related is the truth as I remember it in my writer's heart. The last clause of that statement should be especially noted, as I am the first to admit my memory is imperfect and at times even creative in spite of myself. I am not a historian, and so may have bobbled a date or fact. If so, I apologize, but I did my best. And I may have erred occasionally in recording my personal recollection of family history. If this has happened, again, I apologize.

Finally, if a movie is ever made of this exploit, I insist that Tony Curtis play my father. I am not sure why, but I know it would work.

God bless.